LET ME TELL YOU ABOUT
ALEX

LET ME TELL YOU ABOUT
ALEX

CRAZY DAYS AND NIGHTS ON THE
ROAD WITH 'THE HURRICANE'

JOHN VIRGO

JOHN BLAKE

Published by John Blake Publishing Ltd,
3 Bramber Court, 2 Bramber Road,
London W14 9PB, England

www.johnblakepublishing.co.uk

First published in hardback in 2011

ISBN: 9781843588825

British Library Cataloguing-in-Publication Data:

A catalogue record for this book is available from the British Library.

Design by www.envydesign.co.uk

Printed and bound in Great Britain by CPI Mackays, Chatham ME5 8TD

1 3 5 7 9 10 8 6 4 2

Papers used by John Blake Publishing are natural, recyclable products made
from wood grown in sustainable forests. The manufacturing processes
conform to the environmental regulations of the country of origin.

ACKNOWLEDGEMENTS

My aim in writing this book was to present the serious and lighter side of an extraordinary talent. Alex Higgins made snooker sexy, racy and massively entertaining and changed the face of my beloved sport. He put it on the world stage and made it a game now enjoyed by millions globally. Certainly, there were times when we didn't see eye to eye – but as a colleague and a friend we had some great times. Thank you, Alex, for the ups, downs, laughs and hysteria. The snooker world will miss you, bud.

This book is a true labour of love and would not have been possible without the vision of my publisher John Blake. Thank you for your belief in both me and Alex. Huge thanks also for teaming me up with the highly talented Chas Newkey-Burden. Thank you, Chas, for your time and endless patience. I have learned a lot from Chas and I would like to think he is now a bit of a snooker expert… not to mention a horse racing pundit! I hope we work together again, Chas, I enjoyed our days of reminiscing and pasties!

I had a great time working with the first class team at John Blake Publishing – not least my amazing editor, Lucan Randall. Forever gracious, Lucian worked tirelessly to accommodate my late changes and impossible scrawl and miraculously still got this book out on time!

I am also indebted to many people without whom this book would not have been possible. In particular I would like to thank my dear friends Jimmy White, and Geoff Lomas who knew Alex as well as I did and helped to remind me of some of our times with him. Thanks also to Eric Whitehead, David Muscroft, Roger Lee and Trevor Smith for searching their archives and producing the great photos of Alex.

Lastly to my darling wife, Rosie – the heart and soul of John Blake Publishing – without whom this book would not have seen the light of day. This book is dedicated to her.

CONTENTS

FOREWORD

When Alex Higgins passed away, all of those who knew and loved him were devastated. I was in awe of Alex and I cried all day when I heard the news. It was not just that the sport I love had lost its most influential ever figure — I had lost a much-loved friend and the man who so influenced my game and life.

Alex was a wonderful and sometimes wild man, a much discussed but little understood figure. His potent combination of snookering genius and personal notoriety fascinated the media and the public, but he could also be a guarded and baffling character, so nobody until now has managed to get to the core of who he was.

There is nobody better equipped to write about Alex's life than John Virgo, and no one more qualified to explain just how influential he was in snooker. John was there as Alex made history at the table and made headlines away from the game. Like me, he loved Alex and has witnessed first-hand the highs and lows of this sporting genius.

Alex inspired a generation of people to play snooker. I know – I was one of them. He made the game popular and exciting and single-handedly fired it into the mainstream. The history books might show that he won just two world titles, but the hearts and minds of the public show that he won so much more than that.

For all the controversy that surrounded his life, Alex will never be forgotten. He was a great friend to me and he had the heart of a lion. In these pages, John gets to that heart and shows you what it was really like to work and play alongside Alex Higgins as he revolutionised the game of snooker.

There was never a dull moment when he was around. So sit back and let John tell you about Alex. It's a fascinating story...

Jimmy White

PROLOGUE

I think a lot of us who knew Alex Higgins well suspected he would not live on to a ripe old age. He just always had an aura around him of one who might meet an untimely end. Sadly, our suspicions were proved right. There was an additional tragedy in that our final memories of him were mostly uncomfortable ones. Yet even near the end there were moments of magic from the Hurricane.

I got him involved in a tour of exhibition matches near the end of his life. It proved a testing experience at times. We knew that he had been very ill, but as far as we were concerned he had been given the all-clear from cancer. Well, you wouldn't have thought it to look at him – he had lost *a lot* of weight. He was only on the tour because Jimmy White had been forced to pull out at the last moment due to some ill health of his own.

To think that the promoters had been worried about telling the public that Jimmy wouldn't be there! They needn't have worried, because they had replaced him with a man who was pure box-office to the end. From the first match we did on that tour, the punters were queuing round the block to see him.

Sadly, Alex did not appear to be the Hurricane any more. He was moving so slowly round the table and was clearly a mere shadow of the man he had previously been. The only 'Higgins speciality' he seemed to have remembered was his grouchiness. If someone in the front row of the audience moved while he was lining up a shot he would glare at them. He created this atmosphere, which was actually scary to a point – audience members were terrified to move and everyone felt a bit uncomfortable. But then, in the last frame of an exhibition game in Newport in South Wales, the magic suddenly came back. He suddenly changed – and made a 143 break. The effort he had put into it was just stunning. There was sweat literally pouring off him as he moved around the table. When he reached the 70 mark the audience were suddenly completely behind him to make the 100 break. That is the landmark, after all: any professional wants to make a 100 break. Then he got past the 100 and cleared up; there was a standing ovation for him. The roof nearly came off the place. I was so happy. Could this be the spark of a major comeback for Alex? I dared to wonder. He came over to me and gave me a hug and the emotions were running high for everyone. He was still pouring with sweat, he was drenched. I thought, *That's* why he's still playing. He is a man with so much willpower and effort inside him.

Jimmy played a few exhibitions with Alex after that. Although Alex wasn't up to his usual standards of play, there were still some explosive moments. On one occasion Alex was reaching over to make a difficult pot and Jimmy asked the referee whether Alex had accidentally fouled by touching the blue. The referee agreed and called 'Foul!' Alex walked past the referee and punched him in the stomach. Outrageous behaviour and though there were many times in his life when he could get away with such things, those times had long since passed by now. The referee was not about to stand for being punched. He turned round and grabbed Alex. As the referee held him in a headlock, Jimmy was laughing in the background. Only Alex could get into these scrapes, and only he could have people laughing as he did so.

Then, he, Jimmy and I went to Jersey to do a charity night. The young son of one of the sponsors was sitting in the front row of the audience, fidgeting a bit as he watched. He must have been around seven years of age. Alex missed an important black and decided it was the boy's fault. He walked up to the lad and said, 'If you move again, I'm going to have you shot.' That is just Alex.

Subsequently, we signed up to perform a Legends tour at Sheffield's Crucible, the home of snooker. It was a week before the World Snooker Championship in April 2010. Alex caused trouble with the promoter straightaway, by wanting an extra £250 to wear the waistcoat they suggested. When I introduced him to the crowd he kissed me on the cheek as he passed me. It was quite odd that he did that, considering all the run-ins we had down the years. Naturally, there was rapturous applause for him – but he just couldn't play properly. I was commentating on the proceedings but I didn't say much while Alex was playing. I just found it all a bit macabre – you don't want to watch your heroes like that. This was a man who could once play every shot in the book, but now, put him on a simple black and he would be struggling to screw the ball back two inches. He'd just got no energy or power left. He had been living on baby food for some time, after losing all his teeth during his cancer treatment. It was terrible to watch him at the Crucible and I wasn't surprised when the promoter quickly decided that Alex wouldn't be asked to take any more part in the tour.

His appearance won't stick in anyone's mind as a classic because of the way he looked and the way he played. We always said he was a fighter, but I think in the end he simply gave up. He didn't want to be out in public looking so ill and frail. He really looked shocking by the end. Then there was the fact that he couldn't play the game any more. He was like a boxer coming back to fight long past his prime – and he was doing it only for the money. I thought back to all the wonderful moments Alex had brought to the sport, all those wonderful performances that took the breath away of everyone who watched them. In 1982 he had ruled at the very same venue, but now here he was looking so terribly frail and struggling to produce anything, let alone a moment of magic.

It was all just sad – and that turned out to be the last time I ever saw him play.

But I don't want to remember Alex Higgins that way. I want to remember him in his prime, as the Hurricane, who swept through the game I love and took our breath away. I owe him a lot and so does the game of snooker. Both on and off the table, for better or for worse, he kept us entertained in style until the end.

I want to remember him as the man who changed snooker – and the man who changed my life.

CHAPTER 1

THE RAT PEN

My love affair with snooker started in the house I grew up in, in Salford. We had an airing rack in the ceiling. I noticed that, rather than unfastening it with a normal stick, my parents used a broken snooker cue. I had seen the cue and knew that my father had played the game it was used for. So it sparked a bit of interest in me. What *was* this snooker game, and might it be a fun thing to try out myself? When I was 10, my father bought me a small table to play on. I would never look back. Snooker has been a large part of my life ever since.

I was born in Salford, Greater Manchester, on 4 March 1946. My father, William Joseph Virgo, was a crane driver at the docks, which were just a 10-minute walk from our house on Robertson Street. My mother, Florence, was the sweetest and most loving woman I have ever met. I had a brother, Bill, and three sisters, Marjorie, Barbara and Dorothy. Before I came along my mother also had a daughter, Joan, who tragically died when she was three years old. We were not a rich family by any means – my father's wage in the 1950s was £9.50 per week. Nevertheless, I look back on those days with great affection.

There always seemed to be food on the table, and we had a lovely roast dinner every Saturday and Sunday. You can imagine how, every Thursday night, which was payday for my father, he came home and gave my mother the wage packet. How else could she feed and clothe us as she did? That said, my father must have kept something back for himself, because from the moment they started televising horseracing on a Saturday he would always have a bet. I was just five years old but horseracing became part of my life too – from cheering on my dad's fancies on a Saturday afternoon to occasionally putting a bet on for him in the backstreet bookie's, on the way to school. I never stayed at school at lunchtime. Well, my mother would always cook a hot meal for my father, so I had a choice between school dinners and mother's cooking. No contest.

After lunch my mother would hand me a piece of folded paper, which I knew contained money for me to place a bet for my father as I returned to school. Having placed the bet, I would speed through the rest of the journey back to school, often pretending I was riding Mandarin, or one of the other great horses of the time. I remember vividly the day I forgot to place the bet and then spent an agonising, terrifying afternoon waiting to see if the horse my dad had asked me to bet on had won. Fortunately, it hadn't, but even that didn't stop him giving me a proper rollicking when he found out I'd forgotten. However, he never bet beyond his means, and his life was all about his wife and children. If they handed out medals for supporting your family, he would have had a chest full of them.

I was moving closer to snooker all the time. Although Salford was basically a dock area, it was also a very sporting part of the world. Salford Rugby League Club played a mere 10 minutes down the Eccles New Road. If you walked for 10 minutes the other way, up Trafford Road and across the Swing Bridge, you would reach Old Trafford, which was sporting heaven. At the top end of Warwick Road was Lancashire Cricket Club, and at the bottom end of the same road was where Manchester United, the greatest team in the world, played football. Warwick Road has since been renamed Sir Matt Busby Way, in honour of his achievements for the club. It can only be a matter of time before a similar gesture is made for Sir Alex Ferguson, after all *he* has done for the club.

Like most lads in the area, I absolutely loved sport as a kid. At school I played football, cricket and rugby league. I also enjoyed running and competed in the inter-school sports days. I have always believed that sport is a vitally important force for working-class people, primarily because it gives us

3

the chance to better ourselves. For instance, in my class at school there were 46 pupils. So the chances of our realising our full potential academically were slim. We needed sport as another option – plus, it was lots of fun. I was good at sport as a schoolboy, but not exceptional. I don't think anyone back then would have predicted that I would go on to enjoy a life so dominated by sport. Certainly, nobody could have known that my life would become so entangled with a man who dominated and revolutionised the game of snooker.

All my friends were sports-daft as well. Every night after school it would be one game or another for us. During those long, wonderful summers we played cricket. The games could go on into the evening on a bright day. For the rest of the year it would be mostly football that we played, and only occasionally rugby. The games were contested on an area of waste ground that had been bombed by German aeroplanes during the Second World War. The playing surface was not so much a grassy pitch as a debris-strewn area. Put it this way, you wouldn't want to be diving around where we played, so we played touch rugby, rather than the usual game with its dives and lunges. Still, we always had lots of fun.

Then, one night in September 1958, everything changed. It was a pleasant autumnal evening and I was taken by surprise when none of my pals were on the street corner where we usually congregated. I wondered what had happened, so I went and knocked on the door of my good pal Alan

Heywood, whom we all knew as 'Chinner'. His mother answered the door and said that Chinner and the gang had gone to the billiard hall on Small Street, just off Trafford Road. So I went home and asked my mother if I could go and join them. She said no. Why not? I wondered out loud. She explained that my father believed that billiard halls were 'dens of iniquity'.

That must have been serious, I thought – iniquity was a big word for my dad.

For the next few nights, I continued returning to the Croft and finding nobody there. So I kept asking my mother if I could join my pals at the billiard hall. I wanted to see what it was all about, but most of all I wanted to be with my pals again. Eventually, my mother relented. 'Oh, all right,' she said, 'but don't let your father find out.' I was so excited as I set out to visit this infamous den of iniquity. From the moment I walked in, I fell in love with the place. It was 10p (it was called 2 shillings back then) to join. I took lots of bottles to the off-licence to earn the joining fee. I was 12 years old as I walked through its doors for the first time.

The very first thing I noticed were the dim lights over the tables, which gently illuminated the fine green baizes and the differently coloured balls that sat upon them. There were 16 tables in the hall. When I looked at the way the balls were arranged on each one, it looked like a painting to me. A beautiful painting of a sky perhaps, the sort of sky that, when you gaze at it, you think 'Cor! I'd love to paint that.' That probably sounds like quite a romantic sentiment for a 12-year-old boy to have, but I think that when you find something that really fills up your senses, as snooker did mine, then all kinds of thoughts are possible. Snooker had captured my imagination, and even now, so many decades on, it has yet to release its grip.

So it was love at first sight for me and the game – but there was trouble on the cards for me when my father found out about my new love. To say he was not happy would be an understatement. He was so angry that he stopped referring to the place as a den of iniquity, but began calling it a 'rat pen'. A bit over the top, I thought, but 'rat pen' was easier to pronounce than 'iniquity', at least. So, every cloud and all that. Anyway, I told him I definitely wanted to keep going. He needed a lot of convincing, but eventually succumbed. So I returned triumphantly to the billiard hall – and quickly found myself in such a mess that my father felt all his fears had been confirmed.

I had got to a reasonable standard of play in a short space of time during my visits to the rat pen. Sadly, my youthful exuberance bubbled into overconfidence. One of the characters who hung out at the billiard hall was a man called Jack Scholes. He was a good player, much better than me and my pals were. One night he offered us a challenge: he would play me and my seven other friends and, if any one of us beat him, he would pay for the cost of the lights. Needless to say, he beat all eight of us – though I came closest to beating him. I had to wait until the end of the challenge, and I did not get home until 10.30pm. My father was waiting. He was furious and he gave me a good hiding. I was banned from ever setting foot in the place again. My father very rarely hit me, so when he was so angry with me about the billiard hall I took notice of the punishment. It was many years before I returned to the 'rat pen'.

Indeed, by the time I was next there I was 15 years old and trying to make up for some wasted time at school. I was returning home after an unsuccessful attempt at enrolling at night school. I was not allowed to enrol on the course I wanted to join because I didn't have the required GCE qualifications. Like most of my mates, I thought a GCE was an electrical appliance, so I was not able to enrol on the course. On my way home I walked back into the billiard hall, the place that had so captured my imagination a few years earlier. How happy I was to return to this wonderful place, with its atmospheric lighting. The clicking of the balls was like music to my ears. 'It's good to be home,' I couldn't help but feel. I was back.

For the next few months I secretly returned to the billiard hall many times. As far as my father was concerned I was going to night classes, rather than returning to the rat pen of iniquity. Even once he found out, though, he didn't seem to mind too much. Which was helpful, because my game was improving rapidly – and my skill was beginning to be remarked on. The hall had a new manager, a leading amateur player from Bolton called Stan Holden. He was the first person to tell me I had a real ability at the game. Stan began to teach me the finer points of the game and I quickly improved. Within five months of starting to learn from him I was the Under-16s Boys Champion of Great Britain. So began a journey that would take me around the world, make me a leading light in the game.

Stan had driven me to the Under-16s tournament in Soho Square in London. He gave me some tips about parts of the game, like how to get the best out of a screw shot. It was a memorable journey, not least because the back of the car where I was sitting was full of transistor radios, which Stan planned to try to sell in the capital. I won that tournament and when I came back there were reports of the games in the *Salford Reporter*, but the details of who won were not included, because the paper's deadline came ahead of the final match. Therefore, when I got home my dad had no idea who had won. I proudly told him I had. It felt good.

What happened next was quite surreal, actually. I put the trophy on the sideboard and then there was this strange procession of neighbours who wanted to see it. They would walk through the front door, admire the trophy, shake my hand and then turn and leave through the back door. Then the next edition of the *Salford Reporter* had my photograph in it. Fame! It was a strange feeling. It got even better: a reporter from the *Daily Mirror* wanted a chat with me. I gave a quick interview, and there it was in the next day's newspaper. The article referred to me as 'a debonair young invoice clerk from Salford'. Debonair! I didn't even know what the word meant! Apparently it can mean 'suave or urbane'. I'll settle for that.

Debonair or not, I never thought of turning professional at that stage, but I did begin to work my way up the amateur ladder. I won the boys' championship in 1961, then the youth championship in 1964, and then I was playing in amateur league matches. I was still working at the office, where thankfully I could take the odd day off work to play snooker without anyone screaming the place down. I even represented England at amateur level. But in truth I was a bit bored with the game and saw no future in it. I remember even saying to a pal once, 'I'm going to pack snooker in.' But then Alex Higgins came along and he just fired up something that was inside me that I didn't even realise had been there. Suddenly I found this passion inside me. Funnily enough, that reporter may have described me as 'debonair', but pretty soon other people were saying that I had a chip on my shoulder. I was an angry young man.

Alex Higgins had a measure of anger in him, too. To understand how important Alex was to snooker, you have to look at how sport works. For the public, it is nearly always the characters who make a sport what it is. One of the earliest characters in the game of snooker, was John

Pulman. He turned professional in 1946, the year I was born. Pulman was a snooker sensation – there is no other way of describing him. He became world champion in 1959, breaking the stranglehold on that tournament that Joe and Fred Davis had enjoyed for so long. He then gained a stranglehold on the game himself, which he did not lose till ten years later, when John Spencer beat him in the quarter-final of the World Championship. The following year he put up a tremendous fight and narrowly lost out 37–33 to Ray Reardon in the final.

Pulman's most memorable characteristic was the running commentary he kept up during his own games. He did this to psyche himself up; he was a determined fellow. 'I'm a right bastard when I'm playing,' he said. Although he was joking, he could indeed sometimes be a right bastard. Humour was never far away, though. Once he was playing on a table with cushions that were so dead it was as good as impossible to get good positional shots. 'Well,' he said, 'at least these cushions are stopping the balls falling onto the floor.' He was a real joker and character – no wonder the public took to him. As one of his fans once pertinently put it, 'I'd rather watch Pulman play badly than watch another player play well.' I totally agreed – that was the sort of magnetism he had. As we'll see, I myself found that bringing moments of humour and brevity to the game could prove popular and profitable.

In 1971 there was a tournament in which the best amateur

players in Great Britain competed. It was broadcast on Granada Television. I won that. Then I was asked to present a television series on how to play the game of snooker. I have to be honest: I didn't have a clue how to go about this. So I bought Joe Davis's book, *Snooker for the Complete Amateur*. I studied it and used it as the basis for my television show. Funnily enough, years later I met Joe and he said, 'I've been watching your programme. It was very good and you have some good ideas.' I replied, 'Well I hope so, because it's your book I'm using.' He smiled and said, 'Ah, good thinking.' It was around this time that I first took notice of an amazing young man from Belfast. He would change my life and the game of snooker for good.

There was no professional game worth speaking about this time. It was purely and simply a very small closed shop at this time. Then it started to change when John Spencer and Ray Reardon came on the scene. Reardon was an ex-miner, then a policeman who earned his reputation as a player when he won the police snooker championship. Spencer and he started to play matches and soon people in the game realised that games between these players were more exciting than anything else going on in the game at the time. Before he turned professional, Spencer would take on seven players. He would give them each a 200-point lead. If he overturned that lead and beat them he would get paid, but if he didn't beat them he wouldn't get a penny. It was as simple as that. He invariably did beat them and was soon being taken note of. He was persuaded to turn professional, and so was Reardon.

Not that they didn't face obstacles. Fred Davis, a key player at the time, was quite open about how he felt. 'Why do we need these people?' he asked. I can actually understand where he was coming from on this. There wasn't that much money in the game to go round at the time, so why would the existing professionals want someone else coming into the game? In the end Spencer and Reardon were accepted as professionals. In 1968-69 Spencer at his first attempt won the world snooker championship, beating Gary Owen in the final. The lasting memory from that match was a screw shot played by Spencer from blue to pink, bringing the cue ball back some seven feet. It was that good that Fred Davis had to admit that he and his brother Joe would not have been capable of it. However, Spencer and Reardon were happy to mostly conform to the game as it was at the time. Snooker was then a gentlemanly game played by men in tuxedos and so on.

Then word got round about some exciting developments in an amateur tournament in Bolton. There were teams competing from England, Scotland, Wales and Ireland. In the Irish team – which won the match – there was this young kid called Alex Higgins. Word started spreading round the game about how amazing this Irish boy was. I lived just ten miles down the road in Salford and I heard people saying, 'You wanna see this Higgins, he's a different class.' I was a few years older than Alex at the time and, although I had won some youth tournaments, I couldn't see any point in turning professional. In fact, to be honest I was getting a bit fed up of the game. I felt I was just plodding along and that there was nowhere to go. I couldn't see any future. Not only that, I felt the game was becoming an interference in my life. If I had a day off work I loved going to the snooker hall for a few games. I vividly remember my boss at work calling me to his desk one day and telling me, 'I have to say, John, if you carry on like this you'll end up selling shoelaces in the park. You're not going to get anywhere.' There wasn't much I could say back. I couldn't very well reply, 'Well, actually, I'm going to become a professional snooker player,' because there wasn't a professional game worth talking about at this point. But Alex was about to change all that.

It was really that Bolton tournament which brought Alex to my notice, when he played for the Belfast YMCA team. Stan Holden, who had been at the match, told me that everyone watching had been stunned by the speed that Alex played at. When he had gone into the match, which was two frames on aggregate, his team had been 154 points behind. By the time he came off the table they were in front. There was an even greater signpost to come. After the match, John Pulman, now world champion, presented the prizes and played Alex in a one-frame exhibition game. One man who watched that game said, 'Alex potted Pulman off the table and basically took the mickey out of him.' This was no mean feat, not least because Alex himself admitted he was 'in awe' of Pulman. This was the first time that anyone began to time how quickly a player made a break. Someone would be saying, 'He's just made a century break in three and a half minutes' and people would reply, 'How do you know that? Who's clocking this?' And his game was also no flash in the pan. In 1970 Alex played six money matches and he won every one of them, including the one against the new world champion, John Spencer.

From the very start, Alex polarised opinion. In 1970, some said he would be world champion in two years' time; others said he would simply flash briefly across the sky like a meteor and then blow up. The former school of thought would be vindicated initially, but Alex's life was to become unpredictable after 1972, so perhaps those with the latter theory eventually felt they'd been proved right. Whatever the case, he was certainly an enigma, but the public quickly warmed to him. He sped around the table and made the most outrageous shot selections; his game was a joy to watch. Not only did he make the game itself more exciting, but he also brought added publicity to the sport. This was something it badly needed.

In 1971, Alex started in the qualifying rounds. In his first match he was drawn against Ronnie Gross, who was a former amateur champion. Alex won comfortably, by 16 frames to 5. It had been an amazing performance, not least because, with the 10 am start for the games, the timing hardly suited Alex's lifestyle. As Gross himself said after the match, 'When I heard I was playing Hurricane Higgins I thought I might turn into a bit of a tornado. But I finished up as a slight breeze.' Alex then faced Maurice Parkin, whom he also beat easily, 11 frames to 3. After that match Gross said, 'Alex is a very good player but I can't see him beating Spencer or Reardon – although Rex Williams is coming back and is young enough.' Parkin and Gross were both former amateur champions. What would happen when the stakes rose for Alex?

In the first round proper, he faced Irishman Jack Rea. Alex was again triumphant, but not as convincingly as some of his admirers had expected. His victory was a relatively narrow 19–11. Part of this can be explained by the fact that he had caught Rea on a good day. Indeed, Rea said afterwards that he felt he had played better than he had done since the 1950s. In the other first round, John Pulman, as a former world champion, had beaten Yorkshireman John Dunning 19–7.

Now, Pulman did not just have a reputation as a fantastic snooker player – he was also known as a legendary drinker. I remember playing at the opening of a snooker club some years after he had retired. At the bar afterwards, Pulman signed a bottle of whisky that he had drunk that evening. By the time I left, he was well into a second bottle. When Dunning had arrived at the hotel for his first-round match,

Pulman had offered to buy him a drink. Dunning gratefully accepted the offer. I'm not sure exactly how long that session continued, but one indication is that, after the match the following day, I asked Dunning how highly he rated Pulman's ability at the table. 'I don't know about snooker, but he's a bloody champion drinker,' he told me. In any case, Pulman's victory over Dunning had set up a tantalising quarter-final between him and Alex. Two larger-than-life characters in so many ways were to come face to face.

This would be the biggest task to date in Alex's career. In many ways it would be the first real challenge he would face. He later recalled it, saying that he felt 'wet behind the ears' in comparison with his opponent. Before the match Alex told how he had grown up watching Pulman play. 'He was my first TV idol,' he said. Indeed, so in awe was he that he had always called him not 'John' but 'Mr Pulman' – and now he was to play against him. The match was described by one journalist in particularly memorable terms. '[Higgins] was dashing around the table like a greyhound and going for the quarter- and half-chances while Pulman with his more tactical percentage game was trying to reduce the exchanges to more logical sequences.' But Alex was the one who came out on top – he won 31–23. He knew his opponent did not approve of his 'wild style of play' and he said he could see Pulman 'out of the corner of my eye and he just kept shaking his head in disbelief'.

He had vowed before the game that he would not be

overawed by playing his hero, but would instead attack 'with brute force and scare him to death'. He was pretty much as good as his word. He described himself as 'elated' to have won the game, but he was quick to pay tribute to his esteemed opponent. Pulman returned the compliment and Alex later admitted that he was so pleased he 'partied for two nights' on the strength of the adrenalin rush the win had given him. Having won that game he then marched on to the semi-final, where he faced Rex Williams, the world professional billiards champion, who had surprisingly beaten Ray Reardon 25–23. Would there be more surprises in store when he faced the Hurricane?

You may be wondering why the matches we played were over different numbers of frames. This was due to the fact that the match between Williams and Reardon was played at seven different venues in Scotland. Basically, they would play anywhere if they could get a crowd. A lot of people at the time gave this as the reason for Reardon's shock defeat. But as Williams showed in his next match against the Hurricane, this was no fluke.

I had got to know Alex by this stage and had quickly developed an affection for him. You see, it was very hard not to like him. He was living not far from me, in Oswaldtwistle, near Accrington. I hadn't started practising yet, but the reports I got from a friend – David Briggs – had truly impressed me. Many snooker players play what is known as 'the line-up' when they are practising. You put all the colours on their spots, then add the reds in a straight line down the middle of the table: six reds in between the pink and the black, nine reds between the pink and the blue. You then put the white anywhere you like and, as the phrase goes on *Big Break*, pot as many balls as you can. Ordinary mortals do just that, but Alex always had to go one better. Every time he played the routine, he would try to pot a black off every red. David told me that one day Alex made four maximums. Not real ones, you could argue, but it still took some doing. It also spoke volumes about his cue-ball control and how he could use it in real match play.

I remember one of the first times I met him. I was playing in the final of an amateur competition and Alex was there. He had just turned professional at the time. I thought I knew everything there was to know about snooker – then I saw Alex playing and I was absolutely mesmerised. I thought, Gee whiz! There's more to this game than I ever realised. The shots he was playing were amazing, as was the whole way he approached the game. People had always been very methodical in the past. Their style never really heightened my senses or captured my imagination. Then I saw Alex play and I thought, Bloody hell! It was really, really exciting. It was an experience that changed everything.

Watching Alex gave me a real spur and reawakened my faith in and love for the game of snooker. I realised that there could be a freedom of expression in the game that I had never felt possible before. I started to realise that I could maybe experiment a bit more. Up until then, I suddenly realised, I had felt a little stifled. This was not that surprising. Anyone starting in a sport looks at his or her peers and follows their example. I would watch how they played a shot and how they approached the whole game of snooker.

All of a sudden here was Alex – and he was putting down a completely different canvas from the one that I had been brought up with. Even watching Joe Davis on *Grandstand*, which I did a lot as I grew up, had not prepared me for what I saw in Alex. All of a sudden I was watching someone who was exciting the audience in a way that I had never witnessed before. The atmosphere was simply extraordinary. Alex had single-handedly rekindled my enthusiasm for the game of snooker. I sometimes wonder what course my life would have taken had he not done so, that is how important Alex was to me. I suppose I will never know what would have happened without Alex, but I'm grateful to him for setting me firmly into the world of snooker.

So, I watched every frame of Alex's semi-final match with Rex Williams, which was held at the Co-op Hall in Bolton. The match had been rescheduled three times – much to the annoyance of Alex, who lost some exhibition work as a result – but from a spectator's point of view it was a match well worth waiting for. For my money, this was

19

the best match I had ever seen at this point. Alex was on good form, but I think Williams was better. Alex lost nine frames in the first two days and came close to losing the match. 'I was cocky as hell – which was almost my downfall,' Alex wrote later, adding that, as he fought back, he felt 'sore of ego'. This was a match that had everything: drama, great skill, two wonderful characters. It went to the last day and the very last frame, which Alex won to come out the 31–30 winner.

I shudder to think how many snooker games I had already watched at this point, but none had been as exciting as that semi-final. The contrast was almost frightening, with Alex's gung-ho style up against the more old-school tactics of Williams. One minute you would have Alex running round the table, then Williams, a former world billiards champion, would be up there and would take what seemed like an age to play his shot. In the final frame Williams looked set to win but then missed an easy blue, effectively handing the game to Alex. As he rued afterwards, that blue might have changed the course of his career – and that of Alex. 'Rex was stuffed and I cleaned up' was how Alex remembered it. Equally significant was that Alex was willing to rethink his game plan during that match. Indeed, as Alex admitted, if he had not done that, Williams would have destroyed him.

The players of today have to cope with more instant pressure that was perhaps not there in times gone by.

However, there were no practice facilities at the venue, so each day was like starting afresh. Also then, unlike now, the players were not provided with wet and dry cloths to wipe their hands and cues on. This is something that players now take for granted. Halfway through one session, Alex's cue obviously wasn't to his liking and he was in need of something to wipe it down with. He didn't himself have a cloth, but Williams did. So, while his opponent was busy at the table, Alex reached over and wiped his cue with Williams's cloth. In itself there was nothing overly cheeky about this. He was just using a dry cloth to wipe down his cue, when all was said and done. But what he did next was characteristic of Alex. As he began losing the next frame, he got a bit hot under the collar as he watched Williams clearing up at the table. He leaned across to grab Williams's cloth again but this time he didn't use it to wipe his cue. Instead, he used it to wipe the sweat off his face and his hands. This was how Alex was: give him an inch and he would take a mile.

However, Williams was to have the last laugh – and in some style.

In those days, the players did not have their own dressing rooms. Instead, there was a single room that was shared by the players, officials and any friends they had along on the day. During the first session's interval, in the wake of Alex's use of the cloth to wipe his face and hands, there was a slightly strange atmosphere in the room, as you can imagine. An awkward silence reigned for a while, then Williams turned to Alex to speak to him. 'I don't mind you using my towel,' he said, 'but I should mention that I have a spot of dermatitis on my hands. I do hope it's not catching.' Needless to say, Alex never used the towel again. I thought Williams had been superb in that match. He was unlucky to lose. Some reports claimed that the easy blue he missed in the final frame was the deciding factor. Believe me, though, it was by no means an easy shot. All the same, Alex returned to the table and cleared up to win the game. He then waited to see who he would be facing in the final.

Well, the other semi-final had seen reigning world champion John Spencer faced by the Australian Eddie Charlton. Spencer won the match 37–32, setting up what was in many ways the dream final. John Spencer, the world champion, facing Alex Higgins, the young pretender – great stuff. Since winning his semi-final, Alex had also beaten Jack Rea to become the Irish professional champion. He had performed amazingly in the Irish tournament, which is played in six venues around Ireland. In one of the sessions, Alex hit a purple patch and won all nine frames.

As Rea said afterwards, 'The way he played, nobody could have lived with him. His cue action is very good, but on the long shots with power he throws everything into it. He moves his head, his elbow juts out, he does everything wrong – and yet he knocks nearly everything in.' That was Alex for you: flamboyant, unpredictable and, most of all, brilliant to watch. The ball was rolling, he had the public on his side and was set to go all the way.

The final of the World Championship was to be played at the Selly Park British Legion in Birmingham and would be contested over the best of 75 frames. Most people were sure that Alex couldn't win. After all, Spencer was a great player with a better all-round game than Alex. I didn't have a car, so I didn't go. It was a dramatic final, though, with the tension set up by the fact that Alex had played a money match with Spencer a few days before the final. Although Spencer had won, Alex had inflicted enough psychological pressure on his opponent to set things up nicely for the final.

There was a packed house at the venue, but backstage the organisers were in something of a panic. The country was gripped by a miners' strike at the time and a power cut was expected. They had arranged to get their own generator as a backup for the lights. Luckily, it was not needed.

Spencer was the first to be introduced and he naturally received a great reception from the audience. However, when Alex was called the noise was even greater. Indeed, this was the first time the world heard what came to be known as the 'Higgins roar'. If you were not lucky enough to witness Alex being introduced to an audience, let me tell you that it truly sends a tingle down your back. It is up there with the feeling when the starter lets the horses go at the Grand National. The only equivalent in snooker since has

LET ME TELL YOU ABOUT ALEX

been when Jimmy White comes out to play at the Crucible. Alex, as always, believed that everybody in the venue was there only to see him play and see him win. 'The place was buzzing and so was I,' he remembered.

I cannot say whether Alex's reception unnerved Spencer or not, but I am sure he had never before felt that so many people wanted to see his opponent rather than him. For the first four days of the match the play was very much nip-and-tuck. To be honest, the snooker was a little average at times – but, boy, was the atmosphere exciting! The fifth day started badly for Spencer because a power cut had left him stuck in the lift at his hotel for 25 minutes. This meant that the afternoon session started 10 minutes late. That allowed just enough time for the waiting Alex to pop into the venue's billiard room, make a 111 break timed at just under four minutes, and then return to the main theatre. I sometimes wondered how people calculated these timings for his breaks, but it didn't really matter. The important thing was that they were keeping people interested.

You can bet your life that when Spencer arrived at the venue he would have heard about this latest break from Alex. Spencer certainly had a bad time of it on day five, when he struggled to keep a hold of 'the Hurricane'. Day six was to be the beginning of the end. In the evening session Alex won all six frames. Everything Alex looked at seemed to get potted. That was the sort of rhythm he got into. As Jack Rea had said after facing a similar onslaught

24

from Alex, once he gets into that sort of mood he is simply unbeatable. So it was that he went on to win the game. Alex Higgins, at the age of 22, became the youngest ever world champion, beating Spencer 37–32. That was amazing, but, then, so were the first words of the new champion after the match: 'I shall be world champion for the next five or six years, and when I'm 30 I will retire.' But would it be that simple? One thing was obvious immediately: whatever happened next, it was going to be exciting.

Higgins had changed the game of snooker for ever, you see. As he himself wrote in his book *My Story – From the Eye of the Hurricane*, '[The] fans were dragging chairs, dropping glasses and even walking past us on the other side of the table to go to the toilets. This was not traditional snooker etiquette at all – and I loved it. The venue and the snooker-mad crowd were more than good enough for me. Looking back, this was the moment when everything began to change, not that we realised it at the time. No one could possibly have known that this match wasn't only going to save me, it was going to bring about the rejuvenation of snooker.'

Wise words – and at the end of each day's play he would return to a humble bed-and-breakfast he was staying in near the venue. It was called the Pebbles, but to make it sound more grand Alex would refer to it as 'the Peebles'.

As for the new world champion himself, he quickly learned that once you reach the top you will get more attention, but some of that attention will not be the sort you were hoping for. Questions were asked of him in the wake of his victory. One journalist wondered about his lifestyle and why he so often appeared with a black eye, a cut or a bruise. Sometimes he looked more like a boxer than a snooker player. How many doors can one man bump into? people asked. There was no doubting his class, though. Plus, he had relative youth on his side at 22, a time of life when the body is more resilient. Could he, people wondered, sustain his wild lifestyle under the pressure of being world champion? Every other professional in the game was now determined to snap at his heels and knock him off his throne.

He had promised all along that if he beat Spencer in the final he would throw his hands up in the air and shout, 'I am the greatest.' He was too scared to on the day, but he hoped it would not be long until he won his next title. But *would* he ever repeat his World Championship triumph, and, if so, when? Who knew at that stage that it would take him 10 years to manage it? But there would never be a dull moment during those years. Alex, by winning the title at that tender age of 22, had ended for ever the image snooker had as only an old man's sport.

The way Alex played the game gave it a new, more edgy image. The way he behaved away from snooker was pretty sensational too.

CHAPTER 2

BIG BREAKS, BOW TIES AND TEDDY BEAR WARS

So, how did becoming the world champion change Alex? I was to spend a lot of time with him in the wake of his victory, so I could see at first hand the effect it had. Nowadays, when we think of a world champion, we think of big money and large houses. This was not the case with snooker in 1972. Alex was living in a rented house in Oswaldtwistle. He was alone except for his trophies, of which he already had a few. I was soon to visit this rented house and that was an eye-opening experience I can tell you. As we've seen, it had been an amazing victory that had taken him to the world title.

Everyone who witnessed that performance was transfixed. One friend of mine who watched it even wrote a poem about what he had seen. Admittedly, it wasn't really the greatest of poems, but there had certainly never been a snooker player before in history who would inspire people to write verse. Alex was the youngest ever player to win the world championship. The way he did so was like poetry in motion. It was just unbelievable. People who were there were amazed. I was, too, and my love of snooker continued to be reinvigorated by this remarkable man. Little did I know how close I would become with him in the years and decades to come.

Soon after this the snooker club I was playing in at Salford was closed down. So I started going to one in Chorlton-cum-Hardy. Then Alex walked in one day. I couldn't bloody believe it. He waltzed up to me and said, 'Do you fancy a game?' I thought, Bloody hell, this is the world champion! How many times do you get to play against the newly crowned world champion? So I said, 'Yeah, OK.' I think we must have played more than 60 frames, at £2 per frame. I ended up winning £6 off him. Much more valuable than the money was how Alex influenced my game. He got me playing in a rhythm completely different from how I had played before. Instead of all that ponderous, studious looking at things, I was suddenly playing to a rhythm in which everything seemed to be happening at once. It was just unbelievable. I never actually got the £6 from him. He borrowed a jumper off me that night, too, and I never got back. That's the sort of man he was, but in truth neither of these facts really mattered when compared with what the world champion taught me that day.

I wouldn't say he really changed at all. I do remember his asking me if I could get him any exhibition work. In the wake of my television appearance I had begun to take on quite a lot of exhibition work at around £15 a time. So I asked him how much money he was expecting to get from such appearances. He said, 'Well, if you can get me £25, I'll give you a fiver of it as commission'. This was the world champion speaking, which shows you how little money there was available in the game, even for its top professional. I saw more and more of him after this. He came to the club and played against people. In all honesty, it was hard not to have a soft spot for him. He had a very gentle nature. The only problem was that his mood could turn on a sixpence, as we shall see throughout these pages.

Around this time I opened the Potters Snooker Club in Salford with Geoff Lomas, who ended up managing Alex. He was even best man at Alex's wedding. There was a snooker player from London called Patsy Fagan. The club wanted to put on a challenge match between Alex and Fagan, who, like me, was at this point an amateur player. But Don Slack, the guy who ran the club in Acton, said he wouldn't allow the game to go ahead because Alex had failed to turn up for a previous booking. So I rang Don and said, 'Come on, Don, you know what he's like. He's got a new manager now, his diary is in order. Give him a chance.'

He said he'd let the event go ahead but he wouldn't pay Alex a fee. I said this wouldn't be a problem, because we were all looking to make our money on a side bet, anyway. So Geoff and I went to Alex's flat. He was living in the Blackburn area at this point.

I walked into his flat and I couldn't believe what I saw. Strewn all over the floor were hundreds of telegrams that people had sent him to congratulate him on his World Championship success. Then I looked to the sideboard, where the World Championship trophy was sitting. Then my eyes moved to underneath the sideboard and there I saw a small saucer, with a little bit of cheese on it. I asked him what that was there for. He shrugged and said, 'Oh, I've got a mouse, you know. I like to keep it well fed.' The place was just so basic and chaotic. I couldn't believe that the champion of the world was living in these sorts of conditions and leaving food around for a mouse. It was ridiculous, if a little hilarious too. Alex himself seemed perfectly happy living this way. I mean, he was on the road most of the time so to him I suppose it did not really matter. Presumably, he found a way to keep the mouse fed while he was away from home.

So we carried on arranging the match, which was to take place just a few days before Christmas. We were at the Potters Snooker Club in Salford and we had to get to Acton for the match. So we hired a minibus. Bill Myers was driving it. There was a group of us in there and we had all pooled our money to bet on Alex in the match. It was going to be a two-night affair, the best of 21 frames. There would be 10 frames on the first night and 11 on the second. Having driven down the motorway, we arrived at the small venue to find it packed with spectators, all eager to watch the match. Alex was always a big draw, after all. He found the first night tough going and by the end of the evening he was trailing Fagan by six frames to four. Alex just hadn't played that well. As everyone was leaving Alex made a loud, defiant outburst. 'I'll be back tomorrow,' he vowed. He then pointed at Fagan and added, 'And *he* is going down!' It was like something Muhammad Ali might have said. As we will see in due course, I actually saw a lot of similarities between Alex and the champion boxer.

After this I went back to the hotel with Alex. All of a sudden, as if out of the blue, he had suddenly got a girl on his arm. He was also very much on the vodka. At 3am Alex suddenly appeared at Geoff's hotel room, banging loudly on the door. He then made the most bizarre gesture. 'This is my form, isn't it?' he asked, waving a tampon in Geoff's face. A tad bizarre, I think you will agree. Geoff was disturbed and not a little furious. 'You should be in bed,' he told Alex. 'You've got the second part of the game tomorrow and we've all got a lot of money riding on you.' Alex said, 'Oh don't worry about that, babe. He's got no chance – I'll fucking murder him.' He was confident, but he was probably the only one who was.

In truth, the rest of us were all a little nervous at the venue on the second evening. Well, all of us apart from Alex. He appeared with the same girl on his arm. She stayed at his side throughout the evening. When Fagan was at the table and Alex was sitting down, she was sitting on his knee. He was sitting there casually talking with her and we were all thinking, What's going on here? We've got all our Christmas money on his winning and he's sitting there with some girl! He looked like any other guy in a bar on a pre-Christmas evening. It was as if he had just popped out for a drink and a smoke with his girlfriend.

Meanwhile, Fagan continued to perform well. Needless to say, Alex lost. Consequently, a whole gang of us who had put our Christmas money on him to win had lost our cash. This left us in a terrible situation with just a few days before Christmas. We were sitting trying to work out how we could scrape enough money together to buy Christmas presents for people. Personally, I'd bet around £200 or £300 on the victory, which back in the early 1970s was a lot of money.

He came over to us and said, 'Sorry, babes. But he was a lucky cunt.' So there we all were in the minibus afterwards, ready to drive back up North. The atmosphere in the bus was quiet and dejected, as you can imagine. Alex wasn't with us: he had decided to make his own way back home, and that decision raised no protests from us. For the time being we had disowned him. He's lost us all our money, we thought. Let him go wherever he wants and do whatever he wishes.

As we drove along, one of the passengers turned to Bill, who was driving, and said, 'Bill, you're gone the wrong way. It said M1 that way and you turned the other way.' Bill turned round and said, 'No, I'm going the right way. I just want to pop into London because there's this shop that does the best socks in the world. I just want to get some socks.' So we're all sitting in the back seething, thinking how Alex has just cost us all our money and Bill is driving us all through the middle of London so he can buy some socks!

Overall this had just been another example of the truth about Alex: the only thing you could predict of him was that he was unpredictable. As far as the public were concerned, though, he had truly arrived as a force in the game. These were good times for Alex and for the snooker, too. The best times were under way, thanks to him. Alex had made the public sit up and take notice of the sport like never before. Not that the sport's newfound popularity was *all* down to him. The two other factors were to be colour television and the series *Pot Black*. Snooker on television had till then mostly consisted of a few frames on *Grandstand*, the BBC's flagship Saturday afternoon sports show. In the days of black-and-white television the medium was not perfect for snooker. Though at least during the crossover into the colour television era, we had Ted Lowe's infamous comment: 'For those of you watching in black and white, the yellow is behind the pink.'

It had actually been Ted who first suggested to the BBC that, as colour television was coming into widespread use, a snooker tournament for the top professionals might be a good idea. So, on 23 July 1969, *Pot Black* first hit our screens. It was at first a half-hour programme with just one frame being contested per show in what built into a round-robin format, filmed at the Corporation's studios in Birmingham. However, just as the game of snooker had been for some time, *Pot Black* was a closed shop. Willie Thorne was asked to appear on it because he was considered good-looking. When Willie had hair he looked a bit like the American swimming pin-up Mark Spitz. So that's how Willie got to turn professional. Whether he had the ability or not at the time I am not sure. But he wasn't going to turn down the chance to appear on television, was he? It's where we all wanted to be. The chance of its happening for me seemed slim at the time. I was working hard at the office all day, playing in the snooker hall at night. I travelled to amateur competitions when I could, but I didn't even have a car at the time. It was just a pain, and I began to wonder whether I needed the hassle.

Ray Reardon was the first winner of *Pot Black*. It was an instant success with viewers and the BBC was now aware that snooker on television really could attract a big audience. Alex was not to play much of a part in the show, not least because Ted Lowe was not a fan of the Hurricane. The fact that in his one appearance at the studios Alex had taken a pee in a sink didn't help matters much more. All the same, the show had increased interest in snooker among television viewers. So, in 1973, the cameras were to show the highlights of the World Championship semi-final and final. With 24 competitors taking part in the 12-day tournament, some changes needed to be made. The old system of playing each match in a different venue on one table was not going to be an option any more. So the answer was to play the tournament using a similar system to that used for the tennis during Wimbledon fortnight. There were eight tables in total at the City Exhibition Hall, Manchester, where the tournament was to be held. Two of the tables would be the 'main ones' as far as spectators were concerned, akin to having to 'centre courts'. There were some complaints about the noise that spectators caused as they moved from table to table, but the tournament was a great success overall, heralding the start of the commercialisation of snooker.

For Alex, though, it was to be a mixed experience. In his first match in defence of his title, he had to play the former English Amateur champion Patsy Houlihan at the Exhibition Hall. It was expected that Alex would easily dispense with his opponent and the final score records it that way – Alex won 16–3. However, the statistic showed neither Alex already demonstrating his unpredictable side during the match, nor the controversy that his behaviour sparked. Having won the first session 6–1, he turned up 22 minutes late for the evening session. In later years, as I was to find out to my cost, the rules were changed so that if you were late for such a match you would be docked frames. So under those rules he would have forfeited four frames. But in 1973 there was no such rule, though it may well have been episodes such as this one that prompted the rule change.

When he was introduced to the audience he was greeted by a chorus of boos. No sooner had the booing calmed down than it restarted with a vengeance as he attempted to make an apology. He had, he explained, been trying to clean his white Oxford bags, which had been soiled when he leaned over the table in the previous session. He added that he had also needed to re-tip his cue because it had split. The crowd were having none of it. They were not impressed and neither were the authorities, who, Alex felt, wanted his blood from the off. Even Houlihan was fuming, giving Alex a look 'like a hangman', according to the man himself. 'I try to give pleasure to everyone,' protested Alex, with a hint of desperation in his tone. 'Then let's have some,' retorted one spectator.

To Alex's credit, he did indeed give them some. Within five minutes of play resuming he had the crowd roaring its approval as he pulled off a dazzling break. He won every frame during that evening session. Even when the game was not so exciting, Alex managed to provide pleasure and entertainment for all. Whenever Houlihan needed the rest, Alex would rush and get it for him. He also kept up a regular chat with some of the girls in the tableside seats. When Alex was involved, what was going on in the game did not always matter. He would always provide entertainment one way or another. However, he was not to be successful in his defence of his championship, losing in the semi-finals.

He was drawn against the Australian Eddie Charlton, who was nicknamed 'Steady Eddie'. Alex did not seem himself in the tie, perhaps as a hangover from his previous clash. In that match he had only scraped past Fred Davis 16–14. He did not perform well against Charlton and lost the semi-final 23–9. What I remember most is that every time Alex turned up he would have two women on his arm. Not only that, he came out to play in a bright green suit, whereas it was assumed you had to wear black. He got fined £2,000 – a lot of money in those days – for wearing the wrong suit. He knew he was breaking the rules, he was just trying to make a statement. He wanted to show that he was different from everyone else. He didn't like wearing a bow tie. I remember at a board meeting of the WPBSA (World Professional Billiards and Snooker Association) Eddie Charlton said, 'Us letting him not wear a bow tie is like giving him a 14-point start.'

That may sound over the top, but you should remember that nobody wore a bow tie when practising — with good reason. They were uncomfortable. Furthermore, during matches a lot of players prefer to wear a shirt one size too big, so there is room for movement once the bow tie is added. The exception was Tony Knowles, who used to buy a shirt half a size too small, because he thought it would stop his head from moving. Only Tony could have come out with a line like that! The point is that not wearing a bow tie *was* a physical advantage. As a board we had many run-ins with Alex about the bow-tie issue. At first, if you played an afternoon session you wore a normal suit with a normal tie. But, as manager and promoter Barry Hearn acquired more and more top players, he became more influential. That is the equation in snooker. The top player may have bragging rights, but his personal manager can utilise that power and influence. Hearn came up with the idea that players should start wearing evening suits in all sessions: morning, afternoon and evening. There was a bit of a fuss about it, but I suppose it did make players more smart and impressive-looking.

Alex, though, was having none of this. He didn't want to wear a bow tie and, if Alex didn't want to do something, he didn't do it easily. To be excused from wearing one you needed to have a doctor's certificate. Sometimes he was somehow able to produce such a certificate, but not always. Which is why in those days you sometimes saw him with a bow tie, sometimes not. The confusing thing, though, was that, when he played exhibitions, he quite often wore a bow tie quite voluntarily. Maybe the pressure of competition made him less keen; perhaps he sweated more in competitive matches. Or, just as likely, he was cocking a snook at authority – again. How things have changed since his day! Now you see players who never wear bow ties. Also, and this is perhaps due to the influence of *Big Break*, you see players wearing garish waistcoats. Barry Pinches wears a waistcoat in the colours of Norwich City Football Club, yet Alex was once fined for wearing a green waistcoat. Alex was ahead of his time in many ways.

Actually, the tournament's other semi-final was the more memorable one. The man Alex had beaten in the previous year's final, John Spencer, played Ray Reardon. The match was contested over the best of 45 frames, so, when Spencer led Reardon 19–12, he looked certain to progress to the final. However, Reardon had other ideas. He mounted a great comeback and, for the first time ever in the tournament's history, a player won having been seven frames behind. So the public had been robbed of what many considered the dream final: Higgins versus Spencer. In comparison, Reardon versus Charlton seemed something of an anticlimax. However, a rumour that was circulating did give the proceedings an edge. It was being said that, if Charlton won, the next year's World Championship would be held in Australia. This was unimaginable. The game was just starting to take off in Britain and losing the tournament to the other side of the world would have been a terrible blow. Whether these rumours were true, or just scaremongering, I still do not know. At the time, they got us all squarely behind Reardon, though. As far as we were concerned, he was not just contesting the World Championship, but single-handedly fighting for the future of British snooker.

So, when Charlton won the opening seven frames of the 75-frame final, we were on edge to say the least. Reardon quickly turned around the game, proving that he was a great battler. In the years to come he showed those battling qualities over and over, but few instances were as impressive and dramatic as this one. He gained the lead and then never looked back, winning the match 38–32. Charlton had showed that you cannot win the World Championship by simply waiting for your opponent to make a mistake. No, you had to show some flair and adventure, too. You needed a bit of Alex Higgins, you could say. However, with the international flavour that Charlton had introduced to the mix, he had inadvertently sparked a great feeling of patriotism among British snooker fans. Some 25,000 spectators had flocked to the venue to watch the tournament. For 12 brilliant days, snooker had held centre stage. The game was on the rise.

But what of Alex Higgins? He had failed to defend his

title, or even reach the final. Were the predictions that he would simply be a short-term success, a snookering flash in the pan, prove true? He was certainly always good value entertainment-wise, including in his match against Fred Davis. During that match the roof leaked and the rain came pouring in over the table. 'It was hilarious to say the least,' said Alex accurately. 'I guess they should have anticipated the problem – after all, neither Manchester nor Alex Higgins are exactly famous for being dry.' Everything out of the ordinary that could happen seemed to happen to him. I remember him and Davis standing by the table and Alex was holding an umbrella. Everything suddenly seemed to be happening in the game of snooker and Alex was more often than not at the centre of it. It was as if shoots were springing out of the ground wherever you looked. It was newsworthy, for want of a better word.

Alex had told the media that he had not defended his title because of his new lifestyle of wine, women and horses. He later admitted that the real problem was simply that he was not practising enough. This was in contrast to his earlier days, when he would frequently practise for long periods of time – up to 14 hours on regular occasions. His next chance to prove himself came during a tournament in Canada. The emergence of overseas players such as Charlton from Australia, South African Perrie Mans and Canadian Cliff Thorburn was key to the acceptance of the game of snooker as a world sport. Although snooker was very popular in

South Africa, the idea of playing a tournament there was out of the question, because the country was in the stranglehold of the apartheid era. However, Canada was somewhere with no such problem attached to it. I went on a trip there in 1974, to compete in the Canadian Masters. Among those who also travelled there from Britain were young Midlander (and recent runner-up to Reardon in the 1974 World Championship) Graham Miles, Willie Thorne and Alex Higgins.

The furthest flight I had ever taken before this was to Dublin, to represent England in an amateur international. Technically, Graham Miles was the number two at this stage, having finished runner-up in the recent World Championship. We played in the Canadian National Exhibition tournament. If I had thought it was noisy at the City Hall in Manchester, then I was up for an even louder awakening in Toronto. There were two tables set in the middle of the main exhibition building, with thousands of people moving around all the time. Some would stop by the tables, to inquisitively watch what was going on. You could tell that many of them were wondering just what the game was all about. Even Cliff Thorburn, who was the new Canadian champion, didn't really have so much of a following at this stage. Slowly but surely, as the week went on, more and more people came to sit and watch. It was fascinating to see interest in the sport steadily rising in the country. The fact that local man Thorburn won the tournament was even better. That there were two younger Canadians breaking through, in the shape of Kirk Stevens and Bill Werbeniuk, only added fuel to the growing appeal.

After that tournament, we then moved on to Ottawa. Maurice Hayes, a prominent snooker promoter, had booked another exhibition, but in the main the audiences wanted to see Graham Miles. In Canadian eyes he was the second-best player in the world and the real 'pull'. Alex, naturally, was not very happy about this. He was not being given official number-one billing and people seemed to not know who he was. Trust me, he really was not happy at all, because he was not getting that level of recognition and adulation. For instance, when we went out at night people were not recognising him. So, to feed his need to be adored, he hatched a quick plan. It was a bizarre plan to be honest, but, Alex being Alex, he pulled it off and made it work. When he had been in Australia, he used to date a girl called Cara, whose father was a racehorse trainer. So there he was, feeling a bit unloved in Canada, when he phoned her up. 'I miss you, babe,' he said. 'I'm in Canada. I hate the place. Come over to Canada, then come back with me to Manchester – and we'll get married.' Only he would say that – and only he would pull it off!

She flew over to Canada, where we had been playing games with French Canadians in snooker clubs. One night, we'd had a game of cards and Willie had won about

$80 from Alex, who had a bad night. Willie knew that he would be very unlikely ever to see the money, so he came up with an alternative way for Alex to 'pay' him. We had also visited some funfairs in Canada, where they had a game that captured our imagination in a funny way. You had to throw a quarter-dollar coin and, if it landed on a plate, you won a big cuddly toy. I mean big – they were as big as a fully grown man. Willie and I became fascinated by the challenge of this game. Every day we would show up at the game and throw some coins, but we never had any joy. We just couldn't get them to land on any of the plates. Alex, though, had managed to pull the trick off and was therefore the proud owner of a giant teddy bear. Willie, perhaps suspecting that he would never see the $80 that Alex owed him from the card game, suggested another way that Alex could pay him. 'I'll tell you what, Alex,' he said, 'forget the $80, just give me the teddy bear.' So Willie ended up with a giant teddy bear and I had a huge buffalo cuddly toy, which I had managed to acquire not by landing a coin on a plate but by purchasing one from a lucky winner.

We hadn't heard the last of that bloody toy, though.

Soon after this, Cara turned up from Australia and we all had a real laugh together. We went horse riding and played at exhibition clubs. These were good times and Alex was on great form. One night, the proceedings took on a bawdy edge. The announcer was reading out the scoreline as we went along in English and in French. When I reached 69 points, the announcer said, '*Soixante-neuf*.' I gave him a knowing look and everyone started laughing. Then, halfway through a game, I noticed that my cue was getting a bit sticky. I didn't have a cloth handy to wipe it with, so I decided to wipe it with my tie, which was tucked into my shirt. The audience went wild with laughter; even when Alex was trying to play his shot, they couldn't stop laughing.

It was then that I realised that you didn't always have to play well to entertain an audience, but when I went back to my place you would have thought I had just made consecutive centuries, such was the ovation I received. Maurice Hayes approached me after the match and pointed out that, with my deadpan expression, anything I did that was silly became all the more funny. He said, 'You should try to do that whenever you can.' I am not going to pretend that thinking of something funny to do when you are in the heat of battle is easy, but, thinking back, I recall that many other snooker players did just that to relieve a bit of tension. It works.

Anyway, soon enough the trip was over and it was time for us to go home. When we got to the airport, little could I ever have known what was in store for me over the coming hours. As we were checking in for the flight, Cara noticed the huge cuddly toys that Willie and I were carrying. It must have seemed as if everybody had a large cuddly toy – apart from Alex. She asked him what they were. 'Oh, I had one of them, but I gave it to Willie,' he told her. She couldn't believe what she was hearing.

'What did you give it away for?' she asked. 'I would have loved one of them!' Alex was nonchalant in his reply.

'Well, he said he wanted it for his girlfriend, so I gave it to him,' he said, conveniently omitting the fact that he had given it to Willie in lieu of the money he owed him. She was not happy at all.

'Well thanks very much,' she snapped sarcastically. Then she was off, because she was on a different flight from ours. So Alex, Willie and I got on to our plane, and that was when all hell broke loose between them. Talk about being between a rock and a hard place! That is exactly how I felt, sitting between Willie and Alex as they embarked on the mother of all mid-air feuds.

The announcement went out for us to fasten our seat belts, which was actually very apt advice, as it turned out. Alex turned round with a very serious expression on his face and said, 'Er, Willie, I want the teddy bear back.' Willie asked him what he was talking about. 'I want it back,' Alex repeated. 'Cara's seen it and she wants it. Give me it.' Willie explained that he wasn't prepared to give it back. He had promised it to his own girlfriend and there was no way he was going to go back on that promise.

'Anyway,' added Willie, 'you didn't give it to me. I got it instead of the money you owed me. You owed me $80.'

Alex snarled: 'Yes, I did, but only because you're a fucking cheat.'

'What do you mean?' asked Willie, stunned. 'I didn't cheat! I'm not a cheat!'

'Yes you are,' said Alex. 'Everybody in the game knows you're a cheat.'

And this was just the first two minutes of the 12-hour flight! The argument went on and on.

Alex was drinking and snarling and shouting; Willie was giving plenty back; and I was stuck in the middle, trying to calm them down. I had little success. Twice during the flight they nearly came to blows, which is amazing given that Willie is not a fighter. Alex was leaning over and trying to thump him and I was in the middle holding them apart. Just when I thought things were about to calm down, Alex would stoke the flames. 'I want that teddy,' he'd say. Then it would all start up again.

The cabin crew moved the people sitting round about us into business class. One steward came over and told them that, if they didn't keep the noise down, they would report him to the police ahead of our landing in Manchester. Still, there was no respite. I tried everything I could to calm the situation down. I suggested we forget about the teddy bear and have a game of cards instead. 'I'm not playing cards with him,' Alex would say, quite absurdly, 'He's a cheat!' As a last resort, as the pilot announced that we were beginning our descent to land, Alex tried a new tactic. 'OK, I know what to do,' he said. 'When we land I'll tell customs that the teddy's full of drugs. They'll rip it apart and then nobody'll have it.' He never did, but that was his desperate last effort.

So, whenever I think back to those lovely trips to Canada, I also have the memory of that nightmare journey home. It was horrific. However, even the whole teddy bear incident could not detract entirely from what had been a wonderful trip. For me, it had been a particularly poignant experience. For three weeks I had lived and played like a professional. I had enjoyed the experience and began to consider turning professional. Soon I would indeed take that step, so I would be a fellow professional of Alex and be able to witness at even closer hand his wonderful, if sometimes strange ways.

As I got to know Alex I came to realise that he wasn't exactly shy about burning bridges, to say the least. I remember there was a company called Hazel Grove Music Company and they wanted to create a pool table to cash in on the growing popularity of pool as a pub pastime. They wanted to call their pool table 'The Hurricane' and get Alex to endorse it. For every table they sold with his endorsement they were going to pay Alex a royalty of around £60. This was a *good* financial opportunity for Alex – but, true to form, he managed to blow it.

He went for lunch with some representatives of the company to discuss the deal. Less than half an hour into the

Alex in 1972 after winning the world championship.
© *Trevor Smith Photography*

Above: Alex flanked by Manchester United players Alex Stepney and Stuart Pearson.

Below: Don't look like the fighting kind, do they? At a Park Drive 2000 working men's club competition with John Spencer.

Above: Tough game, this snooker – Alex. © *David Muscroft*

Below: Alex watching Eddie Charlton practice… I don't think so! © *Trevor Smith Photography*

And for my next trick… surely a dove will emerge?   © *David Muscroft*

Alex and his wife in 1979.

Above: Alex and Cliff Thorburn in 1980: ready for battle.   © *David Muscroft*

Bottom left: Alex and Willie Thorne with not a teddy bear in sight!   © *David Muscroft*

Bottom right: Alex and Bill Werbeniuk – if you can't do it on fags and beer, it's not worth doing!   © *David Muscroft*

One of those dark cloud
moments for Alex at the 1981
Embassy World Championship.
© Trevor Smith Photography

Above: Jimmy White and Alex at the Crucible in 1982 playing one of the greatest matches of all time.

© *Trevor Smith Photography*

Below: Showing the usual respect towards the dress code. Alex in Sheffield, 1982.

© *Trevor Smith Photography*

meal, Alex had an argument with the managing director and stormed out of the restaurant. I understand the company went on to sell more than 6,000 tables, but he never got a penny. So he missed out on an effortless windfall, just because of how argumentative he was over that lunch. He really was his own worst enemy.

CHAPTER 3

THE HURRICANE BLOWS HARDER

In 1976, Potters Snooker Club in Salford was up and running. My game was improving all the time and I was practising a lot with Alex. It was only in these practice matches that I fully realised how good he was. Alex truly was a genius: the shots he was capable of playing were unbelievable and, in the run-up to the 1976 World Championship, everyone in the club who had seen him practising was backing him to win the title again. I always remember the 1976 World Championship. It was memorable for so many reasons. Shortly before the tournament began, I played Cliff Thorburn in a friendly match. I had gone to Bolton Snooker Club, where Thorburn was residing and offering to play people for money. I turned up thinking it would be easy pickings, because Thorburn didn't seem anything like the player in England that he had been in Canada. After playing him for two hours during which I won only one frame, I realised that I had misjudged him. In reality, his break building had been of the highest quality and on that form I felt he could beat anybody. I told him so, partly because I was aware that he was considering giving the game up and going back to Canada.

I also told the lads at the Potters Club what I thought of Thorburn's form. They laughed it off as a mere flash in the pan. There was no way, they said, that Thorburn could beat Alex in his first match at Wythenshawe. They were right, but only just. The Canadian gave Alex quite a tough game, which Alex sneaked at 15–14. It had been an electric atmosphere during that match. Thorburn became quite a figure in Alex's career and the Canadian always told the story of when they had first met. It was in 1973, in a London snooker club, and Alex challenged him to £5 a frame. So confident was Alex of victory that he offered Thorburn a 40-point start. Thorburn agreed to play Alex, but would accept only a 28-point start. Anyway, Alex wasn't on form on the day and he lost the match. He could never have won, though, having given Thorburn such a start. I think he realised he had been 'done' in agreeing to that and he never paid Thorburn. Indeed, the episode ended with Alex angrily refusing to pay the money and threatening to throw the ball at Thorburn's head.

In the next round, the quarter-final, Alex was to face John Spencer. This was a repeat of the 1972 final. It was always going to be a tight affair, and Alex ended up repeating his previous scoreline, winning 15–14. So Alex was in the semi-final, where he would face his archenemy Eddie Charlton. It was amazing to see how down to earth Alex was, even as he played in the World Championship. I'd see him in the morning and he'd be drilling a hole in the bottom of his cue, removing a weight and then putting a new one in. Geoff Lomas had just come up to me and said, 'John, have a word with him – he's taking the cue apart!' It was true: there he was, just two hours before the semi-final, drilling a hole in his cue.

'Ah yes,' he'd casually say. 'That's better now.' I'd never even heard of this tactic! To me the cue was like part of your arm: you don't drill holes in it. But Alex? He'd be jiggering about with it, drilling holes and swapping weights.

Anyway, Charlton was a tough nut to crack, make no mistake about that. This was particularly true for Alex, because one of Charlton's best skills was to slow the game down. Taking the speed out of it was a deadly tactic to use against Alex, who, after all, wasn't known as 'Hurricane' for nothing. Charlton, who had beaten Alex the year before, was just the sort of man who could knock him off his stride. However, Alex won the first session 5–1 and left the arena with a huge smile on his face. We had all worried about his chances, not least because of his bizarre drilling just a few hours before, but Alex had proved that our fears were unfounded.

There was such passion behind Alex – everybody wanted him to succeed for the game's sake as much as his. I will always remember the day that Alex approached me with a very determined and serious expression on his slender face. 'I've found the secret, JV,' he told me. I immediately dropped everything and gave him my full attention. After all, I thought, this is bound to be a piece of snooker wisdom he's going to give me. This is bound to be a useful nugget of advice, I thought. One that I can take and use for my own game.

'What is the secret, Alex?' I asked him, feeling as if I were on tenterhooks.

He leaned closer to me with a serious expression still on his face and said, 'It's whisky and milk.' That is exactly the unlikely cocktail that he drank while he was playing – whisky and milk. People watching probably assumed he was drinking just milk.

The atmosphere that greeted his semi-final victory was just amazing. It felt as if everyone agreed that a Higgins-versus-Reardon match would be the perfect final. I approached him straightaway at the end of the match and congratulated him. 'Oh, cheers, babe,' he said nonchalantly.

I always remember that this kid then came rushing up and asked Alex for his autograph. The truth is that Alex couldn't even write his own name. He had drunk so much whisky and milk during the game that, although his adrenalin had kept him going during the match, the moment the proceedings were over the alcohol kicked straight in and he was left so drunk that he just couldn't make the pen obey his commands. As soon as the match was over he just collapsed into a drunken heap.

Anyway, we all had the final we wanted: Higgins versus Reardon. Here Alex faced a formidable opponent, a master tactician and a great champion. Ahead of the match Alex was confident – he even went out for a drink with Reardon the night before the match. Naturally, Reardon was the first to leave the bar. Of course Alex had the slight psychological edge because he had already been playing on the Wythenshawe table, whereas Reardon had been playing his games at Middlesbrough. Reardon was allowed a practice go on the table. Of course, the moment he began playing on the table he demanded changes to it, including a change of cushions and cloth. In my opinion this was a reasonable request. That was not the only great tactic that Reardon used. He loved to leave 'tempters' for Alex. These were opportunities in the play that he knew Alex would find hard to resist, but that would be difficult percentage-wise for Alex to pull off successfully.

There was controversy over the change of cushions and cloth that Reardon had demanded, but to Alex's credit he was clear that he had no problem with Reardon's stance. More trouble was to follow due to the television lighting.

Both Alex and Reardon complained about the glare and dazzle from the lights. The standard for a world final was proving farcical. After missing an easy pink in the middle pocket, Reardon proclaimed, 'I can't see the balls.'

Alex won the first session 4–2, but after the lights were adjusted Reardon wrestled control of the game. He finished 8–5 ahead at the end of the first day. Alex then came back in the next session to lead 10–9. It was game on. Alex was on that sort of form he sometimes hit that could make you scared to blink as you watched, in case you missed something. However, Reardon's tactical game began to tell and at the halfway stage he led 15–11. Consequently, Reardon really taught Alex a lesson in this game and beat him 27–16. We were all very disappointed for Alex, but we couldn't deny that he had given us so much excitement throughout the tournament.

There were changes afoot for me at this stage as well. I turned professional in 1976. My first match at the Crucible was the following year, against John Spencer. As the decade came to an end, we were wondering whether Alex had completely lost the plot. We began to doubt he would ever win the World Championship again. He just wasn't producing the goods at the table and was surrounded by talk of late nights, a wild lifestyle and so on. It really didn't look good for the man.

After the World Championship of 1976, a selected

number of professionals were invited to Pontin's holiday camp in Prestatyn. This tournament was now in its third year and brought together eight top professionals who would play their own competition. This was the last year that I would play in this tournament as an amateur. I had got to the final the year before but had been crushed by world champion Ray Reardon. This tournament was, however, making the game more popular. To be able to match yourself against pretty much the best players in the world was an exciting prospect. I say 'pretty much' because Alex was not there. The Pontin's tournament was the brainchild of Ted Lowe and, because of Ted's involvement with *Pot Black*, the players invited to Pontin's were *Pot Black* players. Alex had played in *Pot Black* only once, during which he had managed to upset someone. So he was never invited to Pontin's. Throughout his career there would be other instances when Alex's behaviour caused him to be banned from tournaments.

In case you haven't already realised, Alex had a great aim when it came to shooting himself in the foot. He was also banned from the World Matchplay Championship, due to some misbehaviour in Melbourne. However, he was to get the last laugh when it came to his being barred from the World Matchplay Championship. The tournament was cancelled at the last minute in 1979. This was partly because the organisers were under immense pressure from the cigarette manufacturer Embassy (who sponsored the World

Championship) and the BBC (who broadcast it) not to use the word 'World' in its title. When it was cancelled altogether at the eleventh hour, the professionals who had been due to compete were disgusted. They had left a fortnight free for it in their diaries and suddenly found themselves having a holiday in March 1979. Alex, though, had his diary filled with engagements and games, so he was laughing all the way to the bank, thanks to his being banned from the tournament.

Still, he yearned to win the big one again. The 1978 World Championship has mostly been remembered for the fine form of Fred Davis, the snooker legend who won three World Championships during his illustrious career. At the age of 64, Davis reached the semi-final – a remarkable achievement. I had played him in the qualifiers and lost 9–8. That was a big blow, particularly as for the first time the championship was televised live from day one. This was a good move. People could watch frame by frame from the beginning and realise that there is a whole lot more to snooker than just potting balls. However, Alex inflicted a slight dent in proceedings when he lost in his first match to Patsy Fagan. This was the second year in a row that he had fallen at the first hurdle. It had been an amazing match, though, and at several points Alex looked good to be the winner. But something – overconfidence many felt – meant he threw the advantage away and lost on the pink in the 25th frame. The overall viewing figures were still high, though, and by the time Reardon beat South African Perrie Mans in the final the game of snooker had a whole army of new and informed, fans. Alex wanted those new fans to see him win another major tournament.

More and more changes were afoot, as the game of snooker became ever more exciting and popular. In the 1979 World Championships they did the draw live on television for the first time. I had won the qualifying matches quite comfortably. I was playing Cliff Thorburn, and Alex was on the other side of the dividing screen playing Terry Griffiths, who had just turned professional at the time. I just kept hearing roars and cheers from the audience watching Alex's game. It was clear that he was playing out of his skin and that he had the audience enrapt. One BBC commentator rated this as one of the best games he had ever seen. At the time I was more bothered about my game with Thorburn. I was at the Crucible – this was my big chance to become the world champion. So I was playing a shot, it was a big and important shot and I had to really stretch to set it up. Just as I pulled the cue back there was an enormous roar that went up from the Higgins/Griffiths audience.

I swear that my heart actually stopped beating. It frightened the bloody life of me.

Fortunately, I was able to withdraw from the shot before the cue touched the ball. But I had been terrified by the sudden din. I think in those days people just didn't realise how offputting it could be to be playing when such applause erupted. I calmed down and returned to the shot and ultimately beat Thorburn. But because Alex was on such great form he increasingly took the mickey out of Griffiths. Inevitably, this began to backfire on him. Griffiths was new to the professional scene but he was a great player. He cleared up every time Alex made a mistake and ended up beating him, after Alex accidentally gifted him an easy red. After that defeat Alex declared he was going to miss tea and instead consume 'something stronger'.

In the semi-finals Griffiths was playing Eddie Charlton and I was playing Dennis Taylor. Rightly or wrongly, I believed the tournament had lost something with the exit of Alex. You have to remember what the attitude in the game was at this stage. We were still trying to sell snooker, still trying to make people watch it. Obviously my first priority was to keep winning so I could be world champion. But I was also trying to sell the game. When Alex went out in the first round, it was as if the tournament had lost something. So, and this is a terrible admission in some ways, I decided that I would try to play like Alex in my semi-final. I have always had this ability to impersonate people, so I thought I would give it a go being Alex in this game. From the shots I was attempting to the speed I was playing at, it was a joke. It really was. I got beaten by Dennis Taylor, who went on to lose to Griffiths in the final. So neither Alex nor his impersonator made the final that year.

But I did make the final of the 1979 UK Championship. Having done reasonably well in the World Championship and then practised more at some holiday camps, I went confidently into the tournament. In my first match, I played Tony Meo. I was 5–2 down after the first session of the best-of-17-frames match. However, after making a 102 break I did not look back. I ran out an easy winner at 9–6. Next up came a quarter-final against the new kid on the block, Steve Davis. He was building quite a reputation for himself and was favourite to beat me. I upset the odds by winning a close match 9–7. Steve and I still talk about the final frame to this very day. Just as I was leaning down to attempt the vital pot, his cue – which he had laid down on the seats – rolled off and crashed to the floor.

Well, you can imagine the look I gave him. Steve has said since that it was the only time he hoped his opponent would *not* miss. I didn't miss, but after an incident involving a sandwich in Sheffield (which I'll explain in Chapter 6) and then this, it showed that poor Steve still had a lot to learn. So, having beaten him, I was into the semi-finals. The line-up was Griffiths versus Werbeniuk and Taylor versus Virgo. This was almost a repeat of the previous World Championships line-up. Griffiths had been at the top of his game throughout the tournament. I actually heard David Taylor say, 'Nobody can beat Terry.' After he beat Bill Werbeniuk 9–3 in the semi-final, more and more people were agreeing with David's assessment.

However, I won my semi-final easily too. I beat Taylor 9–4. This time I was not allowing myself to be distracted by anything other than thoughts of the match. I beat Taylor because I had some old scores to settle there (Alex was out of the tournament). I didn't feel I had to impersonate him or anyone else. I could just be myself, and I beat my opponent hands-down. It wasn't even a race. But Griffiths beat Werbeniuk, so I faced the world champion in the final. The game was played over three sessions in those days; they used to finish it on a Saturday afternoon for the *Grandstand* viewers. I was 11–7 in front ahead of the final session. I was in my hotel room, getting ready for a 2 pm start. Then I got a phone call from one of the tournament officials, asking where I was. I explained I was getting ready and that I would be down in good time for it. The official replied: 'Well that's not good enough, the session starts at 1 pm.'

I was stunned. I was staying in a cheap hotel 10 miles outside Preston, because I had been trying to save money. I jumped into the car and drove down to the venue as quickly as I could. I arrived and was told that, because of my late arrival, I would be deducted two frames. I was the first person ever in the competition to be penalised this way. So now I was leading by only eleven frames to nine and Griffiths quickly drew level to 11–11 before the interval. During the break Griffiths approached me and said, 'It wasn't my idea that you forfeit two frames, John.' Then he suggested we split the prize money. I'm sure he was trying to be helpful and not arrogant, but I was infuriated. I said, 'Hang on, you ain't fucking won yet!' I wasn't bothered about the money, I just had the needle. Perhaps that gave me the edge I needed and I ended up beating him by 14 frames to 13. Quite how I managed that win I am not sure. I was pleased by the victory, though. Due to the roller-coaster that the day had been this was both the best and worst day of my snooker life.

It was good to have a laugh and a joke on the road. It could get quite boring and lonely otherwise. Soon after the 1979 World Championships I went on a trip to Preston, to play in the UK Championship tournament at the Guildhall. I stayed about 10 miles from the venue, along with Henry West and John Taylor. Henry was a snooker manager who looked after, among others, Jimmy White, Tony Meo and me. The players he looked after were known for a while as 'the Magnificent Seven'. Taylor (who was nicknamed John the Arab) was a guy I had met in the Ronnie Gross Snooker Centre in Neasden. He had travelled with me during the summer on occasions, to the holiday camps. He was always a real character and great value on the road.

During one visit to a holiday camp on the Isle of Wight, John Taylor and I arrived early. We ordered a cup of coffee and I began to leaf through the newspaper, hoping to get something good on the horses. We were sitting in the snack bar, which was overlooking the hotel's dance floor hall.

Now, at this particular holiday camp most of the guests were in their senior years. I would guess that the average age was around 60. So, as I took my eyes from my newspaper and looked into the hall, I noticed that there was an aerobics class going on down there. As with any other aerobics class, this entailed the participants moving to music. The difference with this one was that each guest would in turn go to the front and dance, with each of the rest of them following their lead.

I turned back to my newspaper and was unaware of what John was up to. A few minutes later I found a horse that I thought stood a good chance of winning its race. I looked up to tell John about it and he had gone. I looked round and down to the dancehall and – with a mixture of horror and amusement – saw that John had joined the aerobics class. As you can imagine, given the age group of those taking part, the aerobics moves had been on the sedate side with this class. So I was a little worried when John took to the front of the class to lead the proceedings. First he did a few arm exercises and them some hip moves. Everybody followed. Then he took it up a notch and dived onto the floor to do some press-ups. A few of the ladies taking part seemed to think about following, but didn't in the end. The men, though, were straight down onto the floor, joining in with the press-ups. John was quite a fit guy and in no time at all he had completed 10 press-ups.

Next thing I knew he was leaping to his feet and doing star

jumps, complete with hand-claps above his head. Some of the ladies were trying to join in with this, mostly only copying the hand-clap part, admittedly. Meanwhile, I was sitting upstairs laughing my head off. However, some of the men who had gone down to do press-ups found they couldn't get back up again. These were elderly people, who were not as sprightly as John. One of the holiday camp staff came into the room and, when she saw what was happening, said, 'What the hell?' John realised it was time to leave and he did just that. We left swiftly, with me silently vowing to myself never to take my eyes off him again. What a character he was!

He had backed me to win the 1979 UK Championship at odds of 20–1. The problem was that he had placed every penny to his name on this bet. No pressure there, then. A good job I won, really.

As I said, Alex Higgins had a way of getting banned from tournaments and trips. For instance, when we went to India for a special snooker tournament, he didn't come with us. The reason was that the previous year he had made quite a severe *faux pas*. Obviously, India is a very hot country. During an exhibition game Alex removed his waistcoat and threw it to some woman in the audience. This didn't go down well at all, as you can imagine. In some ways the Indians are more English than the English, aren't they? So he was banned. But I was there and I won the

Bombay International tournament. I was very pleased with my form there. I had even beaten Steve Davis in the quarter-final. He had just turned professional and was still wet behind the ears.

Alex was appalled by a lot of what he experienced in India – including a huge cockroach. To be frank, two weeks in Bombay had been quite an experience for me as well. I had just won the UK Championship and Christmas was only weeks away – yet here I was in the heat of India. I have never been as shocked and moved by a country as I was during this trip. The poverty was frightening. Drinking the water could put you in the bathroom for days. As for the air, it seemed so dense at times that I could hardly breathe. Maybe it was a good thing that Alex had not come this time.

I made sure the conditions did not affect my form or confidence and I was proud when I beat Cliff Thorburn in the final, 13–7. I was the Bombay International Snooker Champion – it felt good to say it. In those days, when you went overseas for a tournament there were lots of corporate engagements you could be involved in. In India these included cocktail parties. During the days we would gather round the pool, Del Simons and John Spencer playing backgammon.

Me? I was writing poetry. Yes, poetry. The lad from Salford had been moved so much by what he had seen in India he wrote two poems. One was called 'A Baby in Bombay' and was about an experience I had one night when a man holding a baby approached me and asked me for money. I gave him five rupees and he sat in the gutter, holding this baby. I assume that was their resting place for the evening. The second poem was called 'Bombay: Land of Paradise' and was another indictment of how tough life was for most ordinary Indians. It included a line about how Bombay, though 'like paradise to me' was for its people 'a land of toil, for a little money'. India had quite an effect on me, as you can see. I have never been back, but I would suggest to parents that, if their child is getting a bit out of hand, a visit to India might make them realise how lucky they are.

I arrived triumphantly back in England, full of joy about my win. I flew into Heathrow airport and was met by Henry West, my manager. He told me that he had arranged for me to present some prizes at his snooker club. Unfortunately, I had already made arrangements to go to Manchester. He was not happy about this but as far as I was concerned the thought of going home and seeing all my friends was too appealing. In any case, he had never given me any warning about his idea, despite our having spoken on the phone while I was in India. So home to Manchester I went – prompting a pleasant surprise, which nonetheless sparked a telling confrontation with Alex.

It was just as well that I had decided to head for home, because a surprise party had been arranged for me. I was told I needed to pop to a local hotel for something. As I opened the door to the bar, all hell broke loose. All my family and friends were there. My mother, brother, sisters, Alex and his wife Lynn (whom he married in 1980), Geoff Lomas and many, many more. Immediately, someone pressed into my hand a book of press cuttings detailing my recent tournament wins. On the front of the book was the inscription: UK CHAMP & BOMBAY DUCK. I looked across the bar and noticed there was a big banner unfurled across the wall, which bore the same words. To think I could have gone along with Henry's idea and missed this evening. Later in my life I would be the subject of another surprise tribute — as the subject of the *This Is Your Life* television programme. Even that could not touch this evening, though.

It was a few days before Christmas and I had never felt better. I had money in the bank and I felt as if the world were my oyster as I celebrated with family and friends. I had the trophy from the Bombay International Tournament proudly on display and I noticed that Alex was scowling a bit as he looked at it. We were chatting away at the bar, but I couldn't help noticing that something was troubling him. He had that quality about him — you could almost see the storm clouds gathering above him.

He turned to Lynn: 'Why don't you ever do anything like this for me, babe?'

'Well, if you ever won anything I would!' It was a cutting remark under any circumstances. To make such a remark to Alex would have been a big deal. He left the party in a right huff. I've no doubt that when they got home some feathers began to fly. But I always felt that maybe that was just the kick up the backside he needed. Maybe he sat down and took a look at himself and asked himself why it was that he wasn't winning anything any more.

In life we get motivation in many different ways, and, looking back to that time, I think it did a lot to motivate Alex to greater heights. He had been cruising for too long. Was he going to keep treading water, or really dive in and compete? The latter became the answer. After that episode he started coming to Potters a lot more often and practising hard. In the wake of this, you could say that when he was actually competing, the Hurricane began to blow a bit harder. He won the Padmore/Super Crystalate International in West Bromwich. He had an ear infection but still played well enough to claim the £2,000 first prize after beating Perrie Mans 4–2. He was to star and win more in the wake of that victory. At the start of the 1980s it seemed that new sponsors were suddenly appearing from everywhere.

In one of those events, the Wilson Classic in Manchester, Alex made it to the final, where he lost to John Spencer (who had knocked me out in the semi-finals). Although he did not win, it seemed that Alex was on the way back to his best. Not that he had changed: in the Wilson Classic he had been reported for verbal abuse towards the referee, Jim Thorpe. This was not the first time Alex had let rip at

Thorpe. Six years earlier he had told the referee that he needed to 'read the fucking rule book'. At the Wilson match Thorpe ruled a push stroke against Alex, who, like some observers, felt hard done by. Soon Alex was demanding that the referee check that the black was correctly positioned on its spot. He was fined for his Wilson outburst but he was playing better and was, by his own admission, living more soberly than he had for some time.

Alex was on form, with all the sporting brilliance and other less conventional forms of entertainment that entailed. In the next event he took part in, the Benson & Hedges Masters at Wembley, he also reached the final and got involved in controversy along the way. During the final he complained that his opponent, Terry Griffiths, was standing in his line of shot. There was a record British crowd at this match – a total of 2,323. It was only later that Griffiths revealed that Alex had offered him a deal whereby they would split the prize money 50–50, whichever player won. It was Griffiths who won the match 9–5, topped off by a final clearance of 131. 'Great snooker,' as even Alex was to later admit. Alex was on great form and deserved the win, but Alex's runner-up spot and the sort of mood he was in showed that he was increasingly meaning business.

I remember an incident involving Terry's father that took place after this match. Terry had warned his father not to try to speak to Alex after the match – whatever the outcome had been. However, he did approach Alex and introduced himself. 'Perhaps you could tell your son not to fidget so much when I'm lining up a shot,' said Alex.

Terry's father replied, 'I'm very proud of my son and if you were my son then I would be very proud of you.' Alex's hostility melted away and he burst into tears before grabbing Terry's father in an embrace. Great stuff, really.

Next up, he took part in a new tournament – the Tolly Cobbold Final in Ipswich. In the fifth frame of the final – which he was contesting with Dennis Taylor – Alex lost his rag again. Trailing 3–1 to Taylor, Alex was then penalised when he was adjudged to have hit the red and the black. Alex disputed referee Nobby Clarke's call. He asked Terry Griffiths – who was watching the match – to come and judge the decision. Terry refused, telling the furious Alex that he had been drinking a glass of water at that moment – so the decision stood. He got more and more angry, going 'berserk', according to Taylor, who was accused of being a cheat during Alex's outburst, a completely nonsensical suggestion. As he got more angry Alex even appealed to the audience to back up his claim. Later, Clarke and Taylor reported Alex's behaviour to the WPBSA. They fined him £200.

Alex's next event was the British Gold Cup, in which he brushed aside Tony Meo and then beat Ray Reardon in the final.

So, what was to happen in that year's World Championship? With Alex on this sort of run, could he win the big one? The line-up was now increased to 24 players who would compete at the Crucible. I lost in the second round to Eddie Charlton. Steve Davis beat the reigning world champion Terry Griffiths. Davis was quickly installed as the tournament favourite, but there were more twists and turns to come. He faced Alex in the quarter-finals – it turned into one of the greatest Crucible matches of all time.

Davis made a 136 clearance in the third frame. Then, to take the first session lead, Alex nearly became the first man to make a 147 in the Championship. After 15 reds and 15 blacks, he potted a difficult yellow using side, but failed to get on the green. Typical Alex, he turned to the crowd and said, 'It was my tip, I only put it on yesterday and it isn't played in yet.' He was quite a sight, wearing a purple fedora hat in many of the games. With tip played in or not, he went on to win the match 13–9. He had dispatched the favourite – could he win it?

He faced the Canadian snooker legend Kirk Stevens in his semi-final (the other semi pitched Cliff Thorburn against David Taylor). If anybody thought that Alex's semi-final would be a formality for him, they were to be proved wrong. He took his supporters on a roller-coaster ride. He managed to scrape home 16–13 against the dashing Stevens, who was something of a pin-up and follower of fashion back in those days.

He started the final against Thorburn in tremendous style. Before we knew it Alex had opened up a 5–1 lead.

The game then swung the other way and in the seventh frame Thorburn was the winner, with a break of 68. Then Alex's mood seemed to turn and he started complaining that Thorburn was standing in his line of sight. This was a reprise of his tactic against Griffiths in the Benson & Hedges tournament. In both instances it seemed an unfair accusation. I suppose the trouble came about partly because of Alex's style of play. Whenever you missed a shot with Alex, he would be up and out of his seat like a greyhound out of the traps. This did not really give his opponent a chance to get to his seat. In any case, as with Griffiths, Alex's complaint only seemed to make Thorburn more determined to win.

Going into the fourth and final session they were level 13–13. The pressure – and with it the needle – had grown since the seventh frame. It was even boiling up backstage. I was in the WPBSA room when all of a sudden Thorburn's wife came bursting in. She ran up to Dell Simmons, who was then the contract negotiator, and said, 'Alex has just walked up to Cliff and called him a cunt.' There was outrage, people thought Alex was playing nasty mind games and concluded that this was Alex at his worst again. Anyway, Thorburn went on to win the game – Alex later wrote that the audience was 'disappointed' – and afterwards I approached him in my capacity as a Snooker Association board member.

'Is it true Alex called you a cunt?' I asked him.

He shook his head and said, 'No.' You couldn't always believe what Alex said so it's hard to know exactly what went on. It was this sort of scenario that Alex created in the arena and backstage.

That match was memorable partly because it took place at the same time as the Iranian Embassy siege in London. When the BBC left the snooker coverage for an update on the siege, the switchboards were jammed with complaints. People were more interested in the final of the Embassy World Snooker Championship and after 10 minutes the corporation bowed to their pressure and returned to the snooker.

Alex had been 9–5 ahead at one point but, every time he took a lead, Thorburn clawed back. The drama was relentless. At 16–15, Thorburn was in touching distance of victory but then he missed an easy brown. 'I nearly died,' he said later. Alex returned to the table and it was quickly 16–16. However, Thorburn dominated and won the final two frames – pulling off a 119 break into the bargain. So Alex ended up the runner-up in that match, but he was beginning to show signs of that much-needed thing: consistency.

Then in 1981 Steve Davis won it for the first time. Things were about to change with this new kid in town. Alex loved the game. He lived and breathed snooker. But, as in all sports, someone will always come along to knock you off your perch. Steve Davis was the man who did that to Alex,

74

prompting Alex to admit later on breakfast television, 'Personally, I hate Steve Davis.'

Spencer and Reardon were his contemporaries, but Davis was the man who beat him. Davis was more popular in the game than many people wanted us to realise. Even now that he is past his peak, he remains popular, so he has stood the test of time for sure. He had been gaining momentum for a while, winning the Yamaha Organs Trophy and the John Courage English Championship. No wonder so many people fancied him for the World Championship. Even Alex told *Sportsnight*, 'There is no way I expect to win this year.' He looked weary as he made that prediction, and it proved correct: he lost to Davis in the second round.

Steve Davis had sparked controversy from early in his career, including in relation to Alex. When he turned professional in the late 1970s, he was quickly invited to take part in the *Pot Black* series. 'He has the magic name,' said commentator Ted Lowe, who also acted as a consultant for the series. Davis had turned professional only two months earlier, yet here he was taking part in *Pot Black*. Meanwhile, those overlooked by the series included Patsy Fagan, Alex Higgins and me. Clearly, Alex was the most startling omission. The biggest box office attraction in snooker was rejected in favour of a young player who had been professional for only eight weeks. When he was asked about this state of affairs, Ted Lowe said, 'If you look at his record in *Pot Black*, Alex Higgins has not come off at all. We are trying to build up the game of snooker by introducing new names. The television from Sheffield showed snooker as a championship game, snooker as it should be played, if you like. *Pot Black* has always been forward-thinking. We are trying to get the whole family viewing.'

In my opinion these words did nothing to cover the fact that they had made a big mistake in not including Alex. He had won nearly every major title, so to have an eight-man invitation and for him not to be in it was just simply wrong. This was the beginning of the end of *Pot Black*'s credibility in my eyes. I am a great admirer of Ted Lowe and in later years I was privileged to sit alongside him in the commentary box. But he made little secret of the fact that he did not like Alex. He thought that Alex would drag the game down to a level not acceptable in professional terms. I did not agree with him then but now I am not so sure, as we shall discuss later.

You see, in my eyes Alex brought a new excitement to snooker, whatever his faults. He got the spectators on the edge of their seats and inspired young players to follow his lead. I realise that Alex had something of the rebel about him. I suppose that with that comes a price in the eyes of the authorities and establishment. I understand their take on him but I think they should have looked at the bigger picture. Alex was good for the sport, *very* good in fact. Therefore they should have found it within themselves to focus on the good he brought to the game. Take the game of football. Many people criticised Eric Cantona because of his unconventional attitude, but look what he brought to the game. He did not bring only excitement, but also a sense of leadership as he led the mostly young Manchester United team to success. I took personal delight in that success, of course, as a lifelong United fanatic.

In the same year as Davis's victory, ITV got more involved in the sport. This was the first year that ITV would televise a tournament nationwide. To give their tournament some originality they devised a round-robin format for it. With ITV on board the game was soon to be the most popular in the UK. One of the main reasons, of course, was the resurgence of Alex. This continued when he won the Masters title at Wembley, thanks to a 9–6 victory over Terry Griffiths in the final. There was a flipside to his resurgent form in that the better he did, the more pressure he put on the snooker establishment. He was playing without his bow tie and other players began to follow his example. With the standards of dress in snooker beginning to decline, we decided it was time for action.

Sadly, Alex tended to view these sorts of actions as a direct and personal attack on him. This was not the case. It was believed, and I agreed, that part of the appeal of snooker was the dress and conduct of the players. True, Alex was one of those who offended on both scores, but he was not the only culprit, and we were well aware of that.

For instance, Kirk Stevens wore no bow tie and unbuttoned his shirt nearly down to the waist. The question of whether we came down too hard on Alex, or – as many people would have it – were too soft on him is something I will return to again in these pages.

With the venue sorted out and television interested, 1977 was shaping up to be the start of something big. One problem: there were too many players to take to Sheffield so they had to have a qualifying round. This was a little bit one-sided as the WPBSA decided that of the 16 players that would play at the Crucible, 14 should be seeded. That meant that Willie Thorne, Pasy Fagan, Doug Mountjoy, Roy Andrewartha (who was English amateur finalist in 1976) and myself would have to play down to two.

Geoff Lomas in conversation with me one day said he thought that seeding 14 and only two to qualify was wrong. Geoff explained, when I asked what I could do about it, that I should call an EGM. With my level of schooling I wasn't even sure what a GCE was so an EGM – extraordinary general meeting – sounded like Morse code to me. But that's what we did – we rang all the players that the system was biased against and called an EGM.

Ray Williams was chairman, but even before we got into the meeting there were threats being made. Willie Thorne was upset and when I asked what the problem was, he told me that John Spencer had warned that if he won the vote he would never play in pot black again, something that didn't concern me. I wasn't in that tournament, but Willie was and at that time the world championship was the only tournament open. So the threat was... go against the championship and no more invites.

When I spoke to Spencer about his remark, he said, 'All you and your rebels are going to do is ruin the game.' Yes, that's what they called us – 'Virgo's Rebels'. Actually, it should have been 'Lomas's Rebels', but who cared.

So, amid all this antagonism, the meeting started, I spoke for the so-called rebels. The meeting got very heated and to be fair Rex William the chairman kept a very firm grip. We won by the odd vote. If John Pulman had turned up to the meeting as he had promised we would have lost – it was that close.

CHAPTER 4

1982 AND ALL THAT

In 1982, the year that was to become legendary in the life story of Alex Higgins, Steve Davis returned as the reigning champion and the 'Ginger Magician' was widely fancied to retain the title. There was a lot of expectation on his shoulders, but amazingly he lost 10–1 in the opening round, to a young man from Bolton called Tony Knowles. If there was one thing that Tony never lacked, it was confidence, and in that encounter he matched it with his play. After nine frames he led 8–1, much to the astonishment of us all. Just two frames into the second session the game was all over and Tony Knowles had won. The newspapers went to town on the story, blaming everything from Davis's hectic work schedule to bad management for his surprise loss. In the wake of his exit they made Terry Griffiths the favourite. He did not last much longer himself, losing 10–6 to Willie Thorne. Interestingly, Griffiths said after the match, 'I thought I had adjusted my mind to Steve losing, but when I look back I realised that I hadn't.'

Now I was the new favourite for the tournament, with 9–2 odds on my winning. I remember someone phoning me to tell me I was the favourite. I was playing with extra confidence at the start of the tournament, in part because of the extra buzz that Alex's example was continuing to set me. I was playing my best snooker since 1979. In the first round I had beaten a young man from Grimsby called Mike Hallett.

I had a few days off, so I went to Chester to watch some horseracing action. I was talking to a guy and I said, 'What about this Dawn Johnny in the Chester Cup?' He replied that Dawn Johnny would need the ground to be firm.

'I was at Chester yesterday and the ground's very firm,' I replied. He told me in that case the horse had a great chance. He also told me about another horse, trained by Major Dick Hearn, in a later race. So I slapped a big bet on Dawn Johnny and he came in a 16–1 winner. The winnings I made from the bet were huge, bigger than I would have got for winning the world title in snooker. I also made a tidy profit from a double on the other horse, which won at 100/30. Good times.

The only trouble was the win completely threw me. I

went out the next day to face Ray Reardon and I had totally lost my equilibrium and focus. I ended up losing to Reardon, who was his usual focused self. I couldn't believe I had lost, but I had. In truth, I knew on the practice table before the match even started that something was wrong. I had arrived at the Crucible cool, calm and collected. I was playing the best snooker of my life. But then, on the practice table, I couldn't pot a ball to save my life. I was a nervous wreck. The win on the horses the day before had got my adrenalin going and it was still there, messing with my play. I lost the first session against Reardon 6–2 and, though I eventually got going, it was not soon enough. I lost 13–8. When will I ever learn? I wondered afterwards.

Because I was involved on the committee of the WPBSA, I stayed at the venue even though I had lost. Looking back and putting to one side my own demise, I think 1982 was for me the best championship ever. Tony Knowles eventually lost in the quarter-final to Eddie Charlton 13–11. After beating Davis it was disappointing for him to lose to Charlton. However, Alex was still in the running. One thing was the same from the start to the finish of his career: he believed that he was Alex 'Hurricane' Higgins and that *everybody* in the venue had come to see him. As an opponent, you felt that as well. As soon as you missed a shot the audience would erupt, ready to see Alex at the table. 'Come on, Alex!' they'd cry and the hall would fill with excitement and anticipation. I think Steve Davis had that worse than anyone, because he seemed to play him so often and because they were such contrasts.

The Higgins roar was in effect again.

Alex, still in the tournament, was practising backstage one night on one of the practice tables. After a few hours of this a security man approached him and said, 'Sorry, I'll have to ask you to finish up in a minute. We're closing the building for the night.'

'I'm practising for the World Championship here,' he replied. 'So fuck off!' The security man said that Alex could have another 20 minutes practising, but then he would have to leave for the night. Alex didn't want to leave the practice room and he knew that, if he even popped out for a moment to spend a penny, the doors would be locked and he wouldn't be able to return to the table. So, when he needed the toilet, he urinated into a plant pot right there in the room. As he later argued, they were fake plants in the pot so he 'wasn't being cruel to flowers'. But, still, he wasn't exactly behaving impeccably.

The security man came back to the room, caught Alex urinating and said, 'Right, that's it. You're out of here.' Alex was furious. He grabbed the man's blazer and tore his security badge off it, taking the breast pocket with it. It was not just a physical assault, but a symbolic one as well. There would soon be some ramifications for this, but in the meantime there was more snooker to be played.

In the semi-final, Alex faced Jimmy White. I've known

Jimmy since he was 14, so, although I was Alex's biggest supporter generally, in this game I was really rooting for Jimmy. He's such a lovely lad and I'd watched him come up through the game. I just thought that this was a great opportunity for Jimmy, who won the first four games. Alex's wife Lynn was worried about Alex and approached Geoff Lomas with her concerns. She said she was worried that he was isolated and that there was nothing more she could do to gee him up.

'I'm worried he's going to lose,' she said. 'I'm worried Jimmy's going to murder him at the table.' Geoff suggested that Lynn phone Peter Madden, a jockey who was an old pal of Alex. They were very close and Geoff felt that Madden was the man who could give Alex the support he needed to turn his fortunes around. If you watch any of the footage of the latter stages of the tournament you can see Peter in the front row of the audience, a reassuring and supportive presence for Alex. He was right next to Alex's seat. The contrast between the two contestants was stark. Jimmy looked as if he were hardly out of school, whereas Alex looked older and more suave. First he came out wearing a black satin shirt, complete with lavender-coloured cuffs. Later he showed up in a blue shirt and then an open-necked-shirt-and-waistcoat combo. He was on such form, twitching and performing. He even managed to toss in a few complaints to the referee, John Williams.

Normally I watch the snooker on television backstage.

But for the first time – and the last, as it happened – I sat in the players' boxes for the last five frames. I always thought that television made the game seem too easy. If the camera is right behind the pocket in most cases you know immediately if the ball is going to go in. Sitting in the arena you would not know until the ball has dropped.

Of the two players that evening, Jimmy looked the more composed. When he went 15–13 ahead, just one away from victory, the writing seemed to be on the wall. The fact that Alex won the next frame, with a break of 78, didn't seem to matter. Surely, I thought, that was too little too late. However, Alex has always been an inspirational player. His shot on the blue was mesmeric. His cue-ball action had not always been in control but, when he sank that blue, it was amazing. Even when you watch it back now it is hard to believe he managed it. That shot could almost be his epitaph. There was then an inevitability that Alex would win.

I was there when Jimmy missed what turned out to be a fateful red, handing the table back to Alex. Nobody could believe Jimmy had missed it. But I felt there was no chance that Alex would seize the initiative. 'There's no way he can clean up from here,' I insisted. 'He's gone, I'm telling you. His confidence has gone.' But the thing about Alex was that, when his back was against the wall, he would break loose from all his shackles and go on to almost unbelievably good form. He potted the ball, potted another and then quickly a third. Now, I've heard the word 'genius' used a lot in sport. In fact, in recent times the word has become in danger of becoming devalued because it is used so much. But believe you me: when he got into overdrive he could do things on a snooker table that were just unbelievable. We've all had little bits of magic in our game, but I've never seen anyone do it the way Alex could.

That day the balls were just flying in for him. It was the greatest break in snooker history and I believe there will never be a better one. Ronnie O'Sullivan's maximum break in 5 minutes and 20 seconds was amazing, obviously. But that 69 break by Alex in 1982 was just frightening. He later said that he had been inspired by Muhammad Ali's performance against George Foreman in 1974. He was entitled to make the connection.

Of course, once he had done it we just knew he was going to win the match. He really could not lose from that point onwards. When he had done it he pointed defiantly at the commentary box, as the audience burst into wild cheers and applause. He knew that everything was coming together and he could only go on to win. On that wave of confidence Alex became a snooker genius. He really was a genius. So he won the semi and was in the final. 'I've got the ten-year itch,' he told the BBC. 'There's nothing wrong with my marriage but I've got a ten-year itch for the world title.'

In the final he faced Reardon, who was not at his best that

year but was still the favourite in most people's eyes. After all, he had won all six of his finals, whereas this was Alex's fourth, of which he had so far been triumphant in only one. 'Ray is too good for Alex,' said Eddie Charlton after losing to Reardon in the other semi-final. Not everyone was writing Alex off, though. Reardon had been in the professional game for years. It was over a decade since he last won a major tournament and his best days were probably behind him. He could still trap Alex and slow his game down to knock him off his stride, it was true. But, at the end of the day, to win snooker you have to take your chance when it comes and pot balls. Otherwise you cannot win, whatever other tactics you employ. Reardon was not doing this consistently at this stage.

On the opening day he was wearing a pink shirt with white cuffs and collar. Alex was wearing a dark satin shirt, with a tie and a purple waistcoat. He soon ripped his tie off. By the time the first day was over he had pulled off a break of 118 and was leading the match 10–7. He had said he wanted to win 'for my little girl' and on the early form he looked good to do it. During an interval he told BBC television, 'It would be nice to be the People's Champion again.'

The next day he came out in a green shirt with red collar and cuffs. Reardon accidentally potted a white and that was the beginning of the end for him. Alex really went for it and, as the BBC commentator put it, 'He's going out in a complete blaze of glory here, controversial, temperamental but a terrific talent for the game of snooker.' Victory seemed his. There was a standing ovation when he won.

We will all always remember the scenes that greeted Alex's victory in that final. He was mobbed by friends and well-wishers. All etiquette went out of the window – it was replaced by ecstasy. He beckoned his wife Lynn and their baby daughter Lauren. 'Bring my baby, bring me my baby,' he said through tears. He had been given the trophy but put it aside to embrace his wife and baby. This was an unheard-of gesture at the time and a very iconic one at that. Once more snooker history was being created by the man who, on the table, brought the game out of the billiard hall and into the public eye.

All the snooker lovers in the country were delighted for Alex. It had been a long 10-year wait since his last victory, partly because of the way the game had changed since he first won. As I've said, the way the game was now played so intensively didn't help players like Alex. He could be a bit of a hellraiser, as we all know. Therefore the 17 intense days of competition were a hindrance to him.

Other players were fine with that sort of setup. For instance, Steve Davis used to go straight to his hotel suite and would play Space Invaders. I used to join him for a game sometimes in his suite at the Grosvenor Hotel. I'd think, This is a bit of a different scene from the old days, when players would head straight to the bar and stay there until the early hours of the morning. Davis took advantage of the fact that lots of his opponents were still relics of the previous culture in snooker. They played in the days when competitions were less intensive and when the day's play started later and finished later. After they had played they would go for an Indian or a Chinese, then on to a nightclub for a few drinks. That was the type of people they were. Going to bed at 10 pm for a 7 am wake-up call before preparing for a 10 am start was just not in our nature.

Delighted as we were for Alex in the wake of his victory over Reardon, we still had a small disciplinary matter to attend do: namely the complaint that he had peed in a plant pot at the Crucible and assaulted a security guard. The AGM was the following morning and featured a prestigious cast of characters including Rex Williams, who was the chair, and John Pulman the vice-chair. Also present were Terry Griffiths, Eddie Charlton and David Taylor. It was traditionally held the day after the championship, mainly because most people involved in the game would have congregated in Sheffield for the tournament. It seemed that every time we had a meeting there was a complaint on the agenda to do with Alex. Sometimes it would be a letter of complaint from a referee, saying that Alex had made him look stupid or called him an offensive name. But this time it was something more serious, Alex's behaviour could have prompted a serious disciplinary issue.

Before we could get to Alex's case, there were a number

of other matters to deal with on the agenda, including minutes from the last meeting and then 'matters arising'. We were working our way through these issues when suddenly there was a knock on the door. The door opened and a waiter came in with a trolley. On the trolley were six bottles of champagne, jugs of orange juice and glasses. They were presented to us 'with the compliments of Mr Higgins'. Pulman was a legendary drinker, a champion consumer. When he saw the champagne his eyes lit up. 'Oh, good old Alex,' he said, rubbing his hands with glee. It was only 10 am, but he got stuck into the champagne as we went through the agenda. It should be said that some of those present refused the champagne, largely because of the early hour. All the same, by the time the minutes had been read, three bottles had gone.

Then there was a second knock on the door.

'Morning babes,' said the newly crowned world champion as he came into the room.

We gave him a round of applause for his victory and Pulman in particular thanked him heartily for providing the champagne.

Alex said, 'Listen, there's a lot of press outside and I'm keen to leave and get home with my wife and baby. So, what's the decision here?'

He was told, 'Well, we're going through the agenda bit by bit. We'll get to your case in due course. Why don't you go home? We'll not release any statement to the press about your case until we've phoned you to inform you of the decision first.'

He said, 'You know, it's taken me ten years to win the title again. I'm going to be a great ambassador for the game. This is just what I needed and I'm so happy. Just forget what happened to the security guard. He wound me up, but it's all in the past now. I'm going to turn over a new leaf.' And out he went. We continued going through the agenda and eventually came to Alex's case. There was a real air of understanding in the room. People were saying that after he had waited so long to win the title again, he was probably in high and tense spirits over everything. Perhaps, we increasingly felt, we should not punish him too much for what he had done. Something of a consensus was forming that with his victory he would hopefully become a changed man. Even Terry Griffiths spoke up for him. The tide was definitely turning in his favour, though there was some opposition to the prospect of his attending a forthcoming tournament in Australia.

This was not a huge surprise. Just as Alex had managed to offend the locals during a tournament in India, so had he behaved badly in the past during a game in Australia. The sponsors had banned him from attending a tournament in Australia ever again. I try to be fair, so I asked what he had done. I was trying to fight Alex's corner. I argued that if he was seeded then surely he had to be allowed to compete. 'Well, apparently he pulled a gun on a guy last time he was there,' Eddie Charlton said. Whether it was a real gun or not, I don't know. But I do know that when somebody knocked on his door he appeared with a gun and said, 'I'll blow your brains out.'

'Well, I suppose that is a slight problem,' I conceded.

We carried on discussing Alex's case, when there was another knock at the door. This time Alex appeared with his baby in his hands. You had to hand it to him, he didn't mind pressing people's emotional buttons. 'Look, guys, this is my baby,' he said. 'We need to go home. So what's the decision?' Rex Williams said, 'Alex, we're discussing it now, but I think things are going to be OK for you.' I gave him a reassuring wink to let him know that everything would be all right and out he went. We carried on discussing his case, but little did we know that he was listening in secret from the other side of the door. We were reaching a consensus that we should go light on him. Charlton kept saying, 'I don't care what you agree, but he can't come to Australia.' Things were looking a lot better for Alex than he could have dreamed of. We were close to agreeing that he would face only a small fine and a reprimand.

But then the door suddenly burst open and Alex was back. This time he stormed in like something out of a gangster movie.

'Listen,' he snarled. 'I don't give a shit whether you fucking want me to play or not.' Turning to Charlton, he added, 'And as for you – I wouldn't go to fucking Australia if you paid me. You can stick snooker up your arse!' We sat there stunned for at least a minute, but it seemed more like an hour. And with that he stormed out again. It had been an extraordinary performance. We had been edging close to a light punishment for Alex, then he threw that complication into the mix. The moment before he burst in it looked is if the worst punishment he could be facing would be a fine of a couple of grand and an oral warning. Now, everyone was looking at each other aghast. He had just told us all to fuck off and to stick snooker up our arse. As Terry Griffiths said, 'He's not changed, has he?'

Unfortunately, I had to leave the meeting before it was finished, as I had television commitments in London. As I drove down the motorway I turned on my radio to listen to the news. It was a leading story: Alex Higgins had been deducted ranking points and fined. I thought if ever there was a case of being your own worst enemy, this was one of the most striking examples of it. He had a big self-destruct button. Ranking points are important, so this was a big punishment he had talked his way into. When he won the title in 1982 he wasn't the Alex Higgins who had arrived on the scene in 1972. He was on a downward spiral and he seemed to get a little bit more touchy about it all. For instance, I remember that summer I did a tour with him in Ireland. He was to sign some posters. Alex had a strange payment structure arranged. If he signed with a normal pen he would charge £1, but if he signed with a gold pen he wanted £1.25.

The awkwardness of the 25p change made it difficult in itself. At one of the shows in Ireland there was an announcement at half-time that at the end of the match Alex would sign any of the posters that were sold. Naturally, the audience flocked to the stand to buy posters for him to sign. However, come the end of the match, Alex disappeared. He had left and so had the guy who had sold all the posters. I was then left to face the anger of 200 furious Irish fans who had bought the pictures purely on the understanding that Alex would be signing them. They were irate, and understandably so. This was the sort of thing he was increasingly doing. He seemed to be getting more and more quirky since he won his second World Championship. He wanted almost to live up to the legend that had built up around him in the public eye. For instance, I remember when we were driving through a village in Ireland, not long after Alex had won his second world title. He suddenly said, 'Stop the car!' He got out of the car and walked into a pub. He quickly ordered a half-pint of Guinness and knocked it back in one. Naturally, a crowd would immediately swarm around him, but before they could reach him he would run out of the pub and back to the car. 'Drive!' he would demand, as the crowd stood confused. A lot of his behaviour was very rude, but I found it interesting as well. In fact, I was fascinated to see at first hand just how far he was prepared to go to upset people.

If we were doing a show, Jimmy would make sure that he

booked a driver who would collect Alex on time and drive him to the venue. The trouble was that, if the car passed a betting shop, Alex would have to go into the betting shop. If the car passed a pub, Alex would have to go into the pub. He'd order a pint of Guinness and sit drinking it. Then he'd roll a little joint and smoke it in the back of the car. He didn't really care about time and it was a big job to get him there and on time. This just added to the sense of anticipation in the crowd. They would sit wondering, Is he going to get here? When will he arrive? He would arrive eventually and there would be people standing outside the front of the venue, pacing up and down wondering if he was coming or not.

The truth is that, with a few exceptions, he did always turn up in the end. I think for some people it would really make their night when he finally arrived. The relief and excitement that his arrival would cause was huge. He was an enigma but he was also good box-office: if you put his name on the bill you knew the event would be a sell-out. We always said if you put Steve Davis in his prime in one venue and then put Alex in another two miles down the road, everybody would be at the one Alex was at. He had that entertaining way of playing, which pulled in audiences.

In the wake of his World Championship victory in 1982, Alex and his good pal and sidekick Jimmy White went on a tour of Ireland. Sometimes on these sorts of tours, players would get a bit concerned about payment. After two days in Ireland they were worried about just that. Their driver learned of their fears and worried that, if they didn't get paid, he might not, either. He promptly absconded with the World Championship trophy, which Alex had taken on the trip with him. Eventually, the driver was tracked down at a mobile-home site. The house was surrounded by the Gardaí, who, using a loud-hailer, began negotiations with the driver. He refused to comply and said that he would hand over the trophy only when he was paid for the days he had worked. Alex was there and his response was to tell the Gardaí, 'Storm the place.' With a snarl, he added, 'He's got my cup – it took me ten years to get that back!' Eventually a more gentle approach resulted in Alex offering to pay the driver out of his own pocket and giving him free tickets for his next match. This did the trick, and, with no charges made against him, the driver even continued to chauffeur them for the rest of the week.

When I arrived in Ireland to join them I could see that Alex was looking a little strained. It had probably seemed a good idea to him to go on the trip but once he got there he felt pressure. Even in exhibition matches there is pressure, particularly when you are Alex Higgins – everybody's hero.

The more famous and legendary he became, the more people approached him asking for autographs. I had seen him refuse to give people autographs quite often in the past. Just out of bloody-mindedness, really. Personally, I can remember only once refusing an autograph myself. That was when I was busily putting a bet on at a horse meeting and someone suddenly wanted me to sign their race card. But Alex seemed to get a bee in his bonnet about signing autographs. It all culminated in a very strange story. We were booked to play an exhibition match at Dudley Town Hall, near Birmingham. I went into the dressing room and Alex was putting his cufflinks in. I noticed that 'HH' (standing for Hurricane Higgins) was embroidered on the cuffs of his shirt. I asked him about them. 'Just got it in Hong Kong,' he replied, 'hand-made out of silk – Hurricane Higgins.' I was a bit envious, to be honest. I had never visited Hong Kong at this stage in my life. It was funny watching him as he played that day. He kept adjusting his sleeve in the hope the audience would notice the 'HH' initials. As if anyone could have seen them from that far back.

At the end of the show, as was customary, we went through to sign autographs for the audience. I got my pen out, but Alex got out an ink pad and a stamp. On the stamp it had carved 'A Higgins' in block capitals. I said, 'What's that, Alex?' He replied, 'It's a time-saver.' Then he added, 'Like the shirt, it was made in Hong Kong.' So, as I was busy signing away with my pen, all I could hear from next to me was the sound of Alex's stamp. The fans were a bit confused but in the main they went along with it. Such was the level of fame and the aura he had that people were mostly too scared to complain. One fan did ask Alex if he would consider a conventional autograph, with a pen, in his case. 'No, sorry, babe,' he said. 'I'm only stamping tonight.' Eventually, the stamping stopped. He had successfully used the stamp in every case. I thought this was amazing. I saw at first hand what you can get away with when you are that famous and you've got that much front. People were put out that he wasn't signing for them with a pen, but they didn't know how to react.

However, there's always one who will go against the trend. When we had finished the signing, one guy walked over. 'Alex,' he said, 'I didn't want to ask you in front of everyone else. But my son Christopher thinks you are the greatest snooker player in the world. He won't even go to bed at night until he's watched you play. He loves you. I've got his book here and I've got a pen. Would you please sign it with "To Christopher, best wishes"?' Alex looked around to check nobody else was looking. I could see his mind ticking over. Then he said, 'OK, come here.' He snatched the book and the pen from the man and wrote 'To Christopher, best wishes' and then stamped his name underneath it. The guy was stunned and stormed out. It was amazing – and inventive, too. Later, I asked him why he was using the stamp. 'I just like to keep people on their toes, babe,' he replied with a shrug.

I think this was a preoccupation of his – he liked to keep people on edge around him. He was a lively guy, though. He may have been slight of frame but he was a fearless little fellow. I was in a bar in Puerto Banús in Spain once. It was about 4 am and I had had a few drinks. It had been a great night. Shirley Bassey and Ronnie Carroll had been singing at the piano. Then Alex turned up. 'Hello, JV,' he said. 'Get me a taxi,' he demanded. I asked him why he thought it was my job to get him a taxi. 'You're my chairman!' he said – by then I had taken over from Rex Williams. 'Now get me a taxi!' The cheek of the man was unbelievable.

Sometimes he met his match, though. In the early 1990s, when the BBC wanted to commission a snooker programme called *Big Break*, I was hired to co-present it with Jim Davidson. During a meeting to discuss the show, I put forward the idea of getting Alex on the first show. The producers agreed and checked that such an appearance would not contravene a ban he was under for head-butting a tournament director (more on that later). So, he was booked to come on the show. Jim Davidson was fascinated by the prospect of meeting Alex. He asked me what he was like as a person. 'Well, he's a bit temperamental,' I said. 'He can suddenly turn.' I felt like saying to Jim, 'Well actually, he's a bit like you,' because that would have been true in a sense. But I thought better of it. Anyway, Jim vowed not to upset him and said he just wanted the show to go well. The first show was filmed at Elstree in a harsh winter. There had been very heavy snow. Backstage there were two sections, one for the regular team and another for the guest stars. We knew that Alex had arrived, though, because the moment he did so he ordered two bottles of champagne for his dressing room. He didn't do any rehearsals or warm-up, just waited in his dressing room until the time for his slot. There were a few delays because the audience were arriving late, due to the heavy snow. So Jim decided to pop out and warm them up once they had got there.

He went out and explained what format the show would take and what exciting features and guests would be included. He then unleashed his first joke at the expense of Alex. 'Did anyone see Alex Higgins in the car park?' he asked the audience. 'Apparently someone said he is out there on his knees trying to sniff up the snow through a straw.'

Alex could hear all this, so I became a bit nervous as to what his reaction would be. Sure enough, a message was soon relayed to us from his dressing room. However, Alex is never predictable and so the message was not quite what I had expected from it. 'A message from Mr Higgins,' began the usher. 'He is wearing a waistcoat that he obtained from the Gilbey's store in Savile Row and if he can give the store a mention he will be allowed to keep the waistcoat for free.' When it came to his time, Jim gave him an admiring introduction and he arrived on set to warm applause from the audience.

'Hello, Alex, nice waistcoat,' said Jim.

'Yes, Gilbey's,' said Alex, 'and not the gin.'

Jim lent over, sniffed Alex and said, 'Well, it smells of gin!'

Ouch! But Alex wasn't worried – he had always been clever about working the whole endorsement game. In those days it was hard to get a personalised cue. Nowadays players like Ronnie O'Sullivan can get them made to his own specifications, but back then it was hard to get hold of a decent snooker cue. He knew how to blag a free cue, though. He would say if they gave him a free cue and he won the World Championship with it he would give them a mention on TV. So people were forever trying to press their cues into his hands. Once, when we were playing in Warrington, we left the dressing room and were walking down a dark corridor when Alex suddenly spotted a circular rack of cues. Quick as a flash, he decided that he wanted one. 'Oh, that looks a good cue,' he said. 'I'll have that.' What he didn't realise was that they were all chained to one another. So as he pulled one cue the whole lot came down and made the loudest din when they all clattered into one another. Before you knew it, security came rushing in, flashing light bulbs and shouting, 'What's going on here?' We all legged it outside as quickly as we could. He would do anything for a cue, that man. He was a perfectionist, always in search of the perfect cue and had quite an interesting collection, as we shall see later.

This waistcoat exchange was not the end of Davidson's banter with Alex. He just kept hitting him with cheeky punchlines. A little later in the show he asked him, 'How is your game at the moment?' Alex replied, 'Well, you know,

I had a bit of a problem with the tournament director, so they've put me out to grass.' Davidson pulled an expression of comical bemusement and asked, 'You've been smoking what?' This was a clash of two outspoken titans and on this occasion Jim was in his comfort zone and Alex was outside his. So Jim got away with a lot of cheek. Alex had that frailty that people exploited. In the wake of that show the Gilbey plugging paid off when Alex, Jim and I visited the shop and got a nice waistcoat each. Alex did not make many returns to the *Big Break* studio, though, mostly because he wanted more money than anyone else. We still had all the other top names. The likes of Steve Davis and Jimmy White in particular always made for a good show.

CHAPTER 5

ALEX THE SOCIAL ANIMAL

We used to go to a bar in Manchester called Blinkers, which was a frequent haunt of the football legend George Best. People often talk about George Best and Alex Higgins as two similar personalities, as we'll see later, but the truth is that Best did not like Alex. Lots of people didn't like him, actually. I think we liked him because we could forgive his extreme behaviour and just appreciate the talent – but he tested us to the limit. Jimmy White, by the end of Alex's life, was at the end of his tether with him. We went to Ronnie Wood's once and then three days later Jimmy would get a call from Ronnie's wife, Jo. 'When are you going to get this fucking fella out of my home?' she would stay. It turned out Alex had been there for days; she couldn't get rid of him. He just moved in. He did that with lots of people. He really lived by the 'wherever I lay my hat, that's my home' philosophy. Although he was always on the move he never drove a car. He would travel round the country either being driven by a chauffeur or by train. You can only imagine the kind of mayhem he caused on trains.

As his game declined in the late 1980s there was the infamous head-butting incident. I thought it was wrong at the time and I still think it is wrong now. There had been a sudden issue surrounding drug testing in sport. I was on the board at the time, though I wasn't chairman. We received a letter from the International Olympic Committee that said that if we did not bring in drug testing they would no longer consider snooker a sport. It was signed by their luminaries, including Sebastian (now Lord) Coe. Barry Hearn agreed that we would have to introduce drug testing into snooker. There were confusion and mixed feelings about this, though. We were working-class people. For us drug testing was off our radar. Drug testing does create issues for the innocent. Take Fred Davis. He was still playing the game into his sixties. He actually reached the semi-final of the World Championship at the age of 64 and was still playing professionally at the age of 69. But then because of drug testing he had to stop, merely because he was on a drug for water retention and high blood pressure, which was a banned substance. Other people had issues with beta blockers they were taking, because these drugs were suddenly considered performance-enhancing.

As for Bill Werbeniuk, he was still drinking a lot of alcohol when he played snooker. Indeed, he was drinking so much it was costing him a pretty penny. He decided to try to claim it back as an expense. He argued that because of a hereditary tremor he was on doctor's orders to drink when he played. I doubt any doctor had advised him to drink as much as he did! I knew he was on a downward curve when we were playing in a tournament in Newcastle. He had a bucket with him containing nine cans of lager – and that was just for practice. Likewise, when he was playing in a tournament in Sheffield he would arrange to have six cans of lager delivered to his hotel room in the morning.

I remember when Alex went to a club for an exhibition match and, whatever he did, he couldn't pot a ball. He was having a nightmare. So he said to the referee, 'These balls are rubbish, they need heating up.' The referee called a break and got thinking as to how best to heat the balls up. The only place he could think of was the pie machine. But this was during the interval, so they were using the machine to heat up pies for the audience. So the machine was stacked with pies and in among them were snooker balls being heated for Alex. Only he could have talked someone into doing that, because he made people scared that he would storm off if they didn't do what he wanted.

He had that way of making people do what he wanted them to. He tested people. For instance, we were once sitting round a table and next to Alex was his hairbrush, yet he asked someone on the other side of the table to pass it to him. It was a ridiculous thing to ask, but the guy sure enough got up and passed it to Alex. Also, he didn't drive but he was rarely short of people willing to drive him around, even if they were not being paid for it. As we've seen, people compare him to George Best. It's a comparison I always hear — but he was nothing like Best. For a start, Best had some humility. I knew him. He used to come into the snooker club in Chorlton and watch me play after his training sessions ended. The comparison lives on, though, in the eyes of some. They say that they are the same people because they're both Belfast boys. I'm still not sure what that means, to be honest. Perhaps coming from a big city gives you a certain outlook that the two of them shared.

People can treat you with no respect whatsoever because of who you are. I remember the game-show host Chris Tarrant approaching me at Langan's Restaurant once and he was friendly enough — I was a player in those days. But, once I got a television show in the form of *Big Break*, some of the show-business types were a little off with me. They felt I had invaded their turf. I was at an awards dinner and a pissed Tarrant came over to me and said, 'Hello, Virgo, you talentless tosser!' I'd had a successful career as a professional snooker player and then as a television commentator, and then got a primetime television slot on a light-entertainment show. And Tarrant, the man who first became famous for throwing custard pies on *Tiswas*, is calling me a talentless tosser?

But, you see, Higgins taught us how to cope with being a celebrity. He undoubtedly went over the top a lot, but he still taught us how to deal with it. Fame is not an easy thing to embrace when you've just come from a billiard-hall background. He showed us how to look out for ourselves. Even now people sometimes frown on snooker, but Alex showed us how to respond. People used to say that talent at snooker was the sign of a misspent youth. Well, people rarely say that any more, do they? Alex was full of confidence as a man – a natural star. When we opened the Potters Club, Geoff Lomas suggested I bring in some of my trophies to display behind the bar. So I brought one or two in. They were not the most prestigious trophies or awards, but they brightened the place up and I was proud to have them there. The next time Alex came in he looked at the trophies and offered to bring some of his own in. The next thing you know he has arrived with a whole series of trophies. A bit of one-upmanship perhaps. They didn't last long, though. He got in a bad mood after having a bad run in a kalooki game. He was convinced someone was cheating him. 'You're all cheats,' he declared, 'and I want my fucking trophies back.' He gathered them all up and took off down the stairs. 'Fuck you all,' he shouted over his shoulder as he went. The next thing we heard was a great clanking din as he fell down the stairs, his trophies noisily falling alongside him. Priceless, really.

When you went out with Alex you were always a bit concerned. I was in Canada when I got a knock on my door around midnight. I opened it and there was Alex. 'Come on, JV,' he said. 'I've got us two girls at a nightclub. I've seen them – perfect.' When we got to the bar I saw two girls who looked Alex's type, but they were sitting with two huge lumberjack guys. I asked him if they were indeed the girls and he confirmed that they were. 'You can sort those guys out, can't you?' It was often entertainment when we went out to nightclubs. I remember a time in Middlesbrough. They had a restaurant and he asked me what I wanted to drink after the meal. I said I quite fancied a Tia Maria coffee. 'Yeah, good idea,' he said and also ordered himself an Irish coffee. We finished up walking around this nightclub with half-pint pots of Irish coffee and calypso coffee. We must have looked quite a sight!

Alex liked to gamble and it is fair to say that he was obsessed with the horses, as I have been for so long, too. However, I heard somebody say after his death in July 2010, 'If Alex had twenty grand in his pocket then he'd put it on a horse.' Personally, I've never seen him gamble like that. That said, once Steve Davis started dominating the game he was winning around 30 per cent of the prize money in the game. He really had that stranglehold on the finances of the game – and good luck to him. His success meant he could lead a very nice lifestyle, with decent cars and nice property. The trouble was that this gave a false perception to the public. People thought we were all earning big money from the game, but we really were not. The only way to get serious money in snooker is still to win tournaments, so if you are not doing that you are immediately under pressure at home. It was hard to keep up with the Joneses. For Alex this was especially true, but more with the public. Therefore, he would go out and splash a bit of money about. He was trying to say to the public, 'Yeah, I'm doing well. I've got plenty of money.' When he won the 1982 World Championship he said to the press, 'This will give me financial security for life.'

Funnily enough, though, in bars he hardly had to put his hand in his pocket if he didn't want to. People were very happy to buy you a drink when they recognised you, just to be able to have a chat with you. The only trouble with that was that having bought you a drink they thought they were your best friend and you would be stuck with them all bloody night. Those nights could really drag because you were landed with someone you didn't know and had next to nothing in common with. The holiday camps were the worst for that. The entertainment staff – redcoats and bluecoats, depending on whether you were at Butlin's or Pontin's – got paid very little for their work and they knew that you as a snooker player were being paid quite well to be working there. No prizes for guessing who was expected to pay for all the drinks when we retired to the bar. That said, the reverse could be the case in other situations. I remember nightclubs who would give us snooker stars a roped-off section and then pass us drinks on the house all night. They were just pleased to have some famous faces there in the corner because that was good for the club. So we were given this celebrity status but it was a mixed blessing. For nobody was this more true than Alex. People would approach him in a club or bar with an inflammatory comment just to provoke a reaction from him. I saw the same happen to Jim Davidson a lot.

This made Alex very vulnerable when he was socialising in public. Back in the early days of my career, if I went into a nightclub in Manchester with a couple of successful footballers I would be recognised more than the footballers. I suppose this was because I was wearing the clothing that people knew me for wearing, whereas the footballers were not known for wearing evening wear. As for famous film stars and the like, if they were in a nightclub they would usually have someone at either side of them protecting them from unwanted attention. If you wanted to go and talk to, say, Sylvester Stallone in a nightclub you wouldn't get anywhere near him. Alex never had that protection. He would be just with a couple of normal friends at most. The moment he walked in, this legendary hellraiser, you could feel the atmosphere turn in the venue. There were always at least a few people in there who wanted to see what reaction they could provoke from him. They would often be the bored drunks at the bar, who suddenly perked up when they sniffed the potential for conflict with a famous face. This made me really feel for Alex, because he was so vulnerable when he was out to relax.

As I've said, I got it myself on occasion as well – I still do sometimes, actually. Just very recently I was out with a couple of pals in York. Our train home was delayed, so we had time to kill. We passed a pub but it was absolutely heaving with people, so we tried to find somewhere more quiet. Eventually, we realised there was nowhere else, but I wanted to spend a penny, so we popped quickly into the pub. I walked in and this fella I didn't recognise called me over to him. 'John!' he shouted 'How're you doing, you knob-head?' I swallowed my anger and walked away. But this illustrates how badly people sometimes treat a famous face.

Alex got that sort of thing all the time, and much more intensely. People knew they could get a story for life if they got in a row or a scrap with the notorious Alex Higgins. After all, if Alex got in a fight with someone in a bar that someone would be in the newspapers and would get their 15 minutes of fame. Their name would be up in lights and, unfortunately, these people were everywhere. This made life difficult for Alex. His bread and butter was playing in exhibition matches. At the end of the night he would have an adrenalin rush from the performance and would not feel ready to sleep. Where could he go and be safe from trouble?

There was a strange paradox: he was comfortable in front of an audience of 1,000 people because he felt he had a force field around him, but when he was out socially he was vulnerable and didn't like it. People would come up and ask him the silliest questions, such as 'What do you think of Steve Davis?' What could he say to that? In these situations the worst thing you could do was to let them buy you a drink. All they wanted was to bombard you with questions about the game. You soon learn that, if you put one word out of place, word would rush round. 'Oh, that Virgo, he's trouble.' Alex had a problem with that, and so did Jim Davidson.

He liked the ladies, of course. Well, he was a decent-looking fellow, wasn't he? He also had the gift of the gab and he could pull off a charming or witty line when he needed to. Add to that his fame and the perception that he was loaded, and Alex obviously attracted a lot of attention from the women when he was out. I remember a joke about Stephen Hendry that underlined the attraction that snooker players held for some women. The joke was that he had a new aftershave range called Essence of Leather, because women loved the smell of a wallet. I had witnessed this sort of trend before I was even famous, having grown up in a dock town. I used to go to a bar near the docks; I was only 15 at the time that this happened. The bar was called the Academy and was above the gents' tailors Burton's. A girl at the bar started chatting to me and asked,

'Which ship are you off, then?' She assumed I was a man just off a ship who would buy them drinks all night just for a bit of female attention.

Alex played the field and could be quite incorrigible. We all went out on his bachelor night, and he got the hump with Tony Knowles. 'You've pulled my bird,' he said. We had to remind him that he was about to get married. I suppose he could be a romantic type for a while but only to 'sow the seeds' with a woman. I don't think he had the ability to sustain that sort of behaviour. That was just the type of person he was. He was never going to be the domesticated sort, was he?

I remember when he split up with Lynn and he was living on his own. I'd been out drinking with Alex and Jimmy. When the venue closed Alex said, 'We'll go back to my house.' When we got there he told me he had some snooker cues in the spare room. I went into the room expecting to see a small collection of cues, perhaps in a rack. However, when I walked in I saw that the room was totally bare, apart from the floor, which was completely lined with snooker cues! It was a big room and the entire floor was wall to wall with snooker cues. He suggested we have a game of snooker. I always remember that he came through to play dressed in a dressing gown. But when he sat down he would have his legs wide apart and you couldn't help but notice he wasn't wearing any underpants. The horror of it! So, no, he wasn't much of a domesticated sort. We wondered if he might settle down when he first became a father, but suffice to say he did not. When you went to his hotel room he would always be sitting there wearing just a pair of underpants and socks. I don't know why he kept the socks on, but he always did. Opening your door to a bunch of people while you're wearing just your underpants was strange enough, but the socks got me every time.

Indeed, I always thought he had a very feminine side to him. Not many people saw that in him, but there was a lot more to him than anyone saw. His mannerisms were always very feminine. You see a lot of snooker players now when they have to stretch their leg over the table to reach a shot. Alex, though, took this to a new level. He brought extra panache and style to it; he was like a ballet dancer. His hand movements were also quite theatrical and feminine. He had a softer side and a charming side, but I have to say, having known him for more than 40 years, that those charming moments were very few and far between. More common were the moments when he would say something extremely hurtful to someone. This was again where his feminine side came out. If you are having an argument with a woman and you are getting the better of it, they will bring up something really hurtful from somewhere, just to put you on the back foot. He was a very intelligent man but the way he could speak to people during an argument was harsh. If he was in a bad mood he would find something to say that would strike a nerve with you. In my case, I would

116

usually see these moments coming and turn on my heels and walk away. For those who stayed, though, he could be very hurtful.

He hurt women, too. I remember when he finished an exhibition match and was on a bit of a high after playing well. We went to a club and had a few drinks. He was on great form. By the end of the night he had pulled a girl, so she came back to the hotel with us. Now, the thing is, Alex and I were sharing a room with twin beds. I said to him, 'There's no way I am going into the room with you two.' He was having none of this and said, 'Oh come on, JV.' He assured the girl I was so tired after all the driving I was just going to go straight to sleep. So there am I in the next bed pretending to be asleep while Alex uses every chat-up line under the sun with this girl. It was just constant dialogue. I eventually did fall asleep but I assume that he ended up having sex with her at some point that night. She left around 5 am and as she did so I heard her say to Alex, 'OK, so my brother's wedding is at 2 pm on Saturday in Wolverhampton – are you going to come?' Alex was nodding away and said, 'I'll be there, I wouldn't miss it for the world.' We got in the car and I said to Alex, 'So, are you really going to go to that girl's brother's wedding?' He looked out of the window, sniffed and said, 'Nah, am I fuck!'

There was another story when he picked up a girl and took her back to his hotel. Overnight, some money went missing from her handbag. So when she left his room in the morning she went to the hotel staff and they called the police, who went to Alex's room and accused him of stealing from her. 'I've not taken any money,' he insisted. The police searched the room thoroughly but they didn't find anything, so they left, with Alex telling them to 'fuck off' as they did so. Jimmy saw this scene and went to Alex's room to ask what was going on. 'Well, they've accused me of taking some money from her, but I haven't done that,' said Alex. Then he winked at Jimmy and opened the hotel room window. Outside the window he had dangled one of his shoes using the shoelace. He pulled the shoe in and showed Jimmy that it was full of her money. It's just crazy, really. But, as you have probably gathered by now, we are not talking about a normal person.

Why did we put up with him? It's a very good question. Maybe it was the excitement of going out with him. We were entertained by how outrageous he could be. Say what you like about him and those who knew him could say lots, he was never, ever boring. I met successful and intelligent people who absolutely idolised him. He knew he had these people in the palm of his hand. They loved him and would do anything for him. Before I became professional if he came up to me and said 'I'm playing an exhibition tomorrow night, JV. Can you run me there?' There was never any question that I would say no. It felt like an honour just to be asked. You'd think, I'm actually driving Alex Higgins! You could feel the excitement when you arrived with him. They would all be waiting outside for him, on edge and wondering if he would even turn up. Then, as he appeared, it was as if a wave of electricity had swept through them. 'Oh, Mr Higgins, it's so good to see you,' they would say. As for Alex, he would treat them with total disdain. 'Where's the dressing room? Get me a drink,' he'd say. But then he would perform and the atmosphere in the club would be absolutely electric. The place would be packed, absolutely packed. He would play a special shot and the roar would go up. It was simply magical.

He had little fear. I've seen him roll a joint in front of a policeman. He got away with it. It was at a rock concert. It wasn't that it didn't occur to him not to. He was just being a daredevil and pushing the boundaries. He always wanted to know what he could get away with. He was even more daring backstage at a rock concert on one occasion. He had been to see the Police play after managing to secure a few tickets for the sold-out concert. However, in procuring the tickets Alex's manager had given an informal promise that Alex would go backstage after and play a couple of games of pool with the band and their entourage. After the concert he went backstage and found Sting alone in the dressing room. 'Hello, babe,' said Alex, cool as you like. He asked where everybody else was and Sting told him they were in the next room practising at the pool table for their big match with Hurricane Higgins. Alex turned to Sting and asked, 'Have you got any gear?' Sting got totally the wrong end of the stick and said, 'Yes, we've got some baseball caps and T-shirts left.' Alex sneered: 'No! Not that kind of gear. I meant the kind of gear that goes up your nose!' Sting explained that he didn't use drugs. Alex walked out, shouting 'Twat!' over his shoulder at the bemused rock star.

I was never that privy to Alex's use of cocaine, though we knew that he was taking it. I'm sure that with his personality he would try anything he thought might give him a bit of a buzz. But was he a drug addict? No, no way in the world. I did see him smoking pot now and again. We were in Australia once and I went into his hotel room to take him out to the racing. He was lying on the bed in just his underpants and a pair of socks. He was a very thin man, so he was quite a strange sight dressed like that. There were three joints on the bedside cabinet next to him. 'This is good gear, this,' he said. 'It's Australian bush, babes.' So we tried a bit. To be honest, it just used to make me laugh more than anything. After that we were off to the trot racing. He seemed fine but I was in a total zombie state – the trot racing was like a *Ben-Hur* chariot race in my eyes. He had that tolerance to it that I didn't share.

So, sure, I saw Alex smoke dope and even occasionally joined in. I never saw him take cocaine, though. Not that I am doubting that there was some knocking around in the snooker world. Kirk Stevens freely admitted that he took it and he lived with me for a while but I never saw him take any. But, then, sometimes you just don't notice these things.

I think because of his problem we never saw what Kirk could have become in the game. Jim Davidson admitted he was an alcoholic, but I never saw him that way. I suppose these people have ways and means of doing it privately. I'm more of a binge drinker if anything. I don't need to have a drink regularly but once I get going and get a taste for it, I can really push the boat out. I've been in bars in the early hours of the morning begging them to pour me 'just one last drink'.

He liked a smoke, though, did Alex. When the smoking ban came in at venues, that made no difference to him. He was having a game of cards backstage at an exhibition-match venue and he was rolling and smoking a joint. There was a huge sign next to him saying NO SMOKING but that wasn't going to stop him. He wasn't just breaking the rule: he was doing it with a joint – a double rule-break! He was always up to a bit of mischief. Sometimes it was a bit of harmless fun like that; sometimes it could be less pleasant.

Other figures in the game caused entertainment, though. One time, when he was playing in Derby, Bill Werbeniuk's consumption caused an issue. After every frame, he would go to the toilet and the marker would go and buy Bill another pint from the bar. At the end of the night he was presented with a bar bill and it showed that he had drunk 28 pints of lager. 'There's no way I have drunk that much,' he said. It turned out that he had drunk around 20 pints himself, but every other time the marker went to get him a pint he was having one for himself. When they found the marker he was paralytic with drunkenness, on the floor! The doctor said Bill couldn't go on drinking like this to deal with the tremor, so he would have to go on to beta blockers instead. That's why he was banned from playing, because he refused not to take them. A doctor argued that the medication would be performance-*enabling*, rather than performance-*enhancing*. It was on the IOC banned list because apparently in one of the Olympic sports an Italian doctor had been giving the athletes beta blockers to enhance their performance in the shooting discipline. So that's why it got banned and that's why we lost Bill and lost Fred Davis.

But the people the testers were expecting to catch out actually kept passing the drugs tests. Kirk Stevens, for instance, was a man who freely admitted he was addicted to cocaine, yet he wasn't failing any of the drug tests. So there was a rumour that some American athletes were secretly carrying bags of other people's urine. When they were called to give a urine sample they would simply pour it out of the bag through a tube and would get round the problem that way. To try to counter this, it was decided that from then on the doctor performing the test would have to physically see the sportsman urinating into the pot. Alex was regularly being tested and so, after a particular match that he had won, he was called in for a drugs test.

The doctor followed him into the room, much to Alex's consternation. Not only that, the doctor was absolutely terrified. I've never seen a man so scared in all my life. You can only imagine the abuse that Alex gave him once they were in the room together.

Apparently, Alex was quickly telling the doctor that he would be unable to urinate while he was watching, so he might as well 'fuck off'. I saw the doctor later and he was a nervous wreck. I was upstairs at the time and word quickly came up that Alex had refused to give the sample and had instead head-butted Paul Hatherall, the tournament director. I rushed downstairs with Del Simmons and John Spencer to see what had happened. We saw Paul Hatherall with blood coming out of his head and holding some cotton wool to his eye. I asked where Alex was and Paul pointed towards a room. It turned out that Alex had lost his rag with Hatherall after storming away from the doctor and tripping up in the process, sending his beer flying everywhere.

I went in and saw Ann Yates the assistant tournament director trying to calm Alex down. I decided to try to help out. 'Alex,' I asked, 'what on earth's happening here?' He turned on his heels and stormed towards me. I wasn't going to move out of his way. I thought 'If he hits me, he hits me, but I'm one of the officials, so I'm not moving. He came towards me, swerved around me and slammed his first through the door twice. How he didn't break his hand in the process I will never know. It went right through the double plywood panel. He was, by his own admission later, a man possessed. This is where Alex is at his worst. I asked him again, 'Alex, what on earth's going on here?' He was steaming with fury. 'Every fucking tournament I am being persecuted,' he said. Spencer told him this was not the case. 'No, you're not being persecuted,' he told him. This did nothing to calm matters down. 'Who's talking to you?' sneered Alex. However, he had a killer line lined up. Knowing that Spencer and his wife had never had children, he added, 'And what's the matter with you, eh? Don't you like children?'

It was as low a verbal blow as Alex could have landed and a red rag to a bull as far as Spencer was concerned. The next thing I knew we had Alex and Spencer, two of the greatest snooker players in the world, scrapping on the floor in front of me. It was an unbelievable sight. Alex was eventually escorted from the venue by the police. This was how Higgins was; this was the sheer chaos he could unleash. He was in deep trouble. You simply cannot head-butt a tournament director and expect to get away with it. So he was banned for six months and had ranking points deducted, which took him out of the top 16. Three days later he was asked at a press conference about the episode. Asked whether he could live without snooker, he sneered and replied, 'Well, could snooker live without me?'

The police decided to prosecute him and charged him with 'assault leading to actually bodily harm' and 'wilful damage to a door'. He was fined £200 for assault and £50 for the criminal damage by Preston Magistrates. The hearing by the Snooker Association would prove far more costly. He was fined £12,000 and banned from five tournaments. Ironically, his subsequent test had proved negative. His comment afterwards was typical of him. 'With this type of tribunal there's no right of appeal, so I've decided to accept the punishment and come back fighting.'

Soon afterwards he was interviewed on the *Wogan* show on the BBC. 'I've got a very short fuse,' he admitted. 'But equally, behind the scenes in snooker, there's a lot that goes on within the game that doesn't meet the eye. There's a lot of cliques and bitchiness and, if your face doesn't fit, well, that's the way it is. I feel as if in many ways in my past 12 or 14 years that I've been used and exploited.' To be honest, I felt he had a point.

The lowest blow I remember him delivering to me came when he once asked me which horse I thought was going to win the Gold Cup that year. We were at a tournament in Bournemouth at the time. I told Alex that I thought a horse called The Thinker had a very good chance in the race. 'OK, I'll have £50 on The Thinker,' he told me. I was commentating on the Bournemouth tournament but I was occasionally popping on the radio to hear what was happening at the Gold Cup. I heard there was snow on the course, so I assumed the race was cancelled and I didn't bother putting a bet on it for either me or Alex. Next thing

I knew I heard that the race had gone ahead and The Thinker had won at 9–1. All of a sudden there was a knock on the commentary room door. It was the snooker player Jim Meadowcroft. He said, 'Alex would like to know when he can collect his winnings.' I explained that I hadn't put the bet on. I was very sorry and I was as gutted as anyone to have missed out. Later, I saw Alex in the hospitality area and he asked me where his winnings were. I explained again that I hadn't had a chance to put the money on because I thought the race wasn't going ahead.

'You're a fucking liar,' he said to me with a snarl on his face.

'No, I'm not a liar, Alex,' I replied. 'I'm gutted myself. I didn't have the bet.'

He then decided to press the nuclear button.

'How's your son?' he asked, fully knowing that, having split up with the boy's mother, I had not seen Gary for a while. I looked Alex carefully in the face and said, 'If you say one more word, I'm going to throw you through that fucking window.'

He quickly said, 'Cheat!' and then raced out. I went after him, fuming. He turned round and laughed at me. He knew I was telling the truth; he was just winding me up to get a reaction.

Alex's ban after the head-butting incident had a number of repercussions. After the World Championship he played Steve Davis in the Masters tournament. Nobody expected him to win, but he did. At the end he was absolutely jubilant.

'I'm back! I'm fucking back!' he cried. That was included in the BBC broadcast of the match, prompting complaints. At the next meeting of the Association this matter was brought up, in light of the complaints. I made the point that this was a highlights programme, so there had been no need for the BBC to include Alex's outburst. I asked the executive producer why he had not edited the outburst out of the highlights package. 'Well, it's a story,' he said. But they had not had to show it, so therefore the complaints were surely the BBC's problem, not the Association's. I suppose I could understand their rationale in keeping it in: after all, for some people the biggest appeal of Alex was his tantrums, his unpredictability. And, after all, he *was* back. Beating Davis proved that. He was fined £1,500 for that outburst, which I thought was a bit severe.

Alex always seemed to be in a league of his own when it came to attention-grabbing behaviour. Whether you like it or not, sport thrives on controversy and also on contrasts between competitors, particularly a sport with just two competitors at any one time, such as snooker. I've watched all of snooker's best and observed their ways.

Now I will turn to how each of them compared with Alex.

CHAPTER 6

ALEX AND ...

For all the fuss that rightly surrounded Alex's 1982 World Championship victory, and for all the entertainment he brought to the game, the fact remains that his two World Championship wins do not compare well with the records of other top players. Steve Davis and Ray Reardon both won it six times. Stephen Hendry has won it seven times. Why Alex didn't do better than he did in his career also brings into focus why Jimmy White, for instance, never won the World Championship. I remember April 1979, when Jimmy first won the English Amateur. He was only 16 and I had first seen him play two years earlier. The thing I noticed first was his natural way of playing and his tremendous *temperament*. If he was 60 points behind and there were 61 left, you could bet your life he would clear up, such was his poise under pressure. Couple that with his amazing cue power and cue-ball control and it became quickly obvious that here was a young man who would go right to the top.

In Jimmy's case there were a few obvious, specific reasons. Missing a crucial black against Stephen Hendry was one of them. But the main reason is that 17 days is a long time for a tournament. Alex had played snooker for two solid weeks. As I said, he was on the whisky and milk. He had this roller-coaster experience of highs full of adrenalin followed by the comedown. Then he would need to get up again for the next match. Reardon, for instance, would not have approached a tournament in that style if you paid him to. He was sauntering through the other half of the draw in Middlesbrough and arrived for the final fresh. Alex arrived absolutely exhausted. When Jimmy White made his maximum break at the Crucible, I was commentating on that match. I went down to Jimmy's dressing room afterwards and his manager told me that Jimmy had already returned to his hotel. I phoned the hotel and they would not put me through. 'No calls for Mr White,' the receptionist told me. I explained who I was but they said it didn't matter who I was. They had been told not to put any calls through to Jimmy and that was the end of the matter.

So I went back to the hotel, went straight to my room and ordered a bit of room service. I was settling in for a quiet night alone. Then at around 11 pm the phone rang. It was

Jimmy. He said, 'I can't sleep. I've just won £147,000. Do you want to go out for a drink?' I said, 'Go on, then.' It was understandable he couldn't sleep: he was on a natural high after an incredible achievement. I couldn't have slept in his shoes, either. So we met up and went to a nightclub we were familiar with. We sat and had a drink and that was that. We didn't overdo it and we weren't out late. But then the rumours start circulating about Jimmy being out all night and returning to his hotel room at 3 am. It was easy for these misunderstandings to happen. On another occasion a rumour went round that Jimmy had been spotted arriving back at his hotel room at 7 am. But that was a misunderstanding.

What had happened was that the starting time for matches had become much earlier in recent times. But there were lots of players, myself included, who just were not used to starting at 10 am. We were used to the matches beginning in the afternoon. There was no way we could roll out of bed shortly before 10 am and go and perform. So what a lot of players – including Jimmy and I – used to do was set the alarm and get up early, perhaps even 5 am or 6 am. We would then go on a walk around the streets of Sheffield for some fresh air, to wake ourselves up. It was worth getting up at the crack of dawn just to have some decent time between waking and playing. So when people saw Jimmy returning to his hotel room at 7 am looking dishevelled they assumed he was just coming in from a night out. But in reality he had just got up.

The point is that when people ask why it took Alex ten years to win the World Championship again after his first victory my answer is that it would not have taken so long had it been continued to be played under the same sort of format as in 1972. In the old days you played someone, then you had a week's rest before you played someone else. That suited Alex's lifestyle. But at the Crucible it was a 17-day intensive slog of living and breathing the game. It made it very hard work for people like him and Jimmy.

Meanwhile, Alex was still attempting to emulate his golden years of 1972 and 1982. Until Jimmy White came along we never had a comparable star to Alex. Jimmy has always been a quite remarkable player, he really, really has. I've known him since he was a kid and I've always been impressed. As a youth he became the youngest player to win the English Amateur Championship in Cornwall. I remember a whole bunch of us piling into a minibus to drive down to the tournament. The great thing that Jimmy has is his temperament. It is just unbelievable. Apart from natural ability, you've also got to have a good temperament to succeed in snooker. I'll be honest and say that my temperament was my big problem. I blew hot and cold. Alex's was the same, actually, and that was our weakness.

On the other hand, Jimmy's temperament – particularly when he was young – was wonderful. If you left him a couple of reds and all the colours – bang, they would all be gone. He had that great ability that saw him win the English

Amateur Championship and then the World Amateur Championship in Tasmania. He was the youngest player to win it. He will admit, though, that just like Alex he would sometimes go for that one shot too many. They get the feeling they are invincible. They see a difficult shot and think, Well, if I just get this one in, I've won the frame, instead of analysing the percentages and being more realistic. Alex wasn't good at that until his latter days and neither was Jimmy. I remember in Cornwall that I noticed for the first time how casual and adventurous he could be. You simply do not get consistent results taking on that sort of shot. Moving forward to today, I think that, if you look at Ronnie O'Sullivan, you'll see he has perhaps gone too far the other way and become too cautious. There is a line between defence and attack. Alex was on the attack side of that line, and so has Jimmy been a lot of the time. Neither of them seemed to win any match easily; they always made it difficult for themselves.

When I am asked who is the greatest player I have ever seen and if I were to answer that question on the basis of temperament then the answer would be Stephen Hendry. When it comes to temperament he is just unbelievable – head and shoulders above everyone else. I have seen him play shots under pressure that simply amazed me. Knowing the game inside out as I do and understanding the pressure he is under, I can see how amazing it is. But you wouldn't know it from outside – he makes it look simple. He just floats along and it seems so effortless. The harder you hit a ball, the more accurate you have to be. The slower you hit it, the better chance there is of its going in, thanks to gravity. However, if you do miss a slow shot you are more likely to be leaving it on a plate for your opponent. It never entered his head that he would miss it. That's why he won so many tournaments. His temperament was spot on. Poor Jimmy kept finishing runner-up, and that was in part because his temperament was not as good as it had been.

Still, Jimmy always remained popular, didn't he? The public love him. This was mostly because the one thing Jimmy never did, however disappointed he felt, was complain. He would be graceful in defeat and would keep his head up, and he shook his opponent's hand. I can only once remember seeing him react petulantly. It happened a couple of years ago. I could see the sheer frustration in Jimmy after he missed a simple shot. In a fit of fury he whacked the white off the table. He knew it would cost him the frame but he was so angry he didn't care. You could hear the crowd gasp in shock. I approached him afterwards and gave him some advice. 'Don't go down that road, Jimmy,' I told him. 'People love you because you never complain. So don't go down that road.'

Alex was the opposite. He was forever complaining and coming up with excuses: the balls were wrong, the authorities were hounding him. He never felt far from an outburst. He had a tirade of reasons for why he had not performed at his best. And that pressure was ruining his game. Jimmy never did that, though. The public noticed that and appreciated it. They don't want to hear excuses or complaints if you have been beaten or played badly. He has grown frustrated at times and behind the scenes he will let off steam. Why shouldn't he? It has to come out somehow and I feel that the right place for that to happen is in private. He also has to face the frustration of people endlessly asking him if he will ever win a World Championship. I've personally lost count of the number of times I have heard him asked this. When we've been doing signings together the question keeps coming: 'Jimmy, will you ever win a World Championship?' It must drive him insane. His stock answer is, 'Yeah, I could still win it.'

With the unwieldy number of professionals in the game, they now play games in an academy in Sheffield. In the arena where these qualifiers are played, you are allowed only a few guests. There is no audience. Can you imagine when people like Jimmy White, who have become used to the adrenalin rush of playing to a packed house, play there? Even Alex, after he had punched a tournament official called Colin Randall, ended up so far down the rankings that he was playing in these small venues. I got the feeling that, even when he was playing well, he wasn't enjoying it. He needed the buzz of an audience around him. Having just few people watching didn't give him that. He really struggled with that, and Jimmy is currently struggling with the same thing. Who can blame them? I don't care who you are, as a sportsman you need the buzz of an audience. It does put pressure on you, for sure. But players like Alex and Jimmy enjoyed that pressure. It brought the best out in them, which is why Jimmy is finding the qualifying rounds so hard. It's a Catch-22 situation for Jimmy. He dropped out of the top 32 and ended up struggling in the qualifiers.

Alex thrived on the adulation of a crowd. When he got out of his seat to play it was for him like walking on stage. Can you imagine how terrible it must have been for him to walk on stage in front of a few people? He missed the adrenalin rush and it showed. When people ask me if I got nervous before I played I always said that without at least a little touch of nerves you are not going to perform at your best. Basically, you can end up a bit too complacent – and that can be deadly to your hopes. In the 1979 World Championship I thought I had won it. I honestly did. I believed there was no way that Dennis Taylor could beat me. But I was wrong.

I also often get asked how I think Alex would have done today if he were playing in this era of snooker. It is very difficult to compare eras, of course. I believe Alex would have had to toe the line a bit more and put more work and practice in. In his day there were only two or three tournaments of note each year; the rest was just exhibition play. There was not that regular opportunity to hone your competitive senses. So, if he had been playing more recently, he would have played through a time when there were more like eight tournaments per year. He would probably have been a better player, too, and won more tournaments. When he moved to a tournament after a prolonged period of exhibition matches it would take him time to get into the flow of it and really warm up properly.

As I said, Steve Davis came along at a perfect time. The likes of Reardon and Spencer had just passed their peak and were approaching their sell-by date. Higgins was even closer to that. Davis was the first dedicated professional in the game of snooker. I remember playing in the world open for amateurs and professionals. Spencer, who taught a lot to Alex's game, was there. He got knocked out early and I went to commiserate with him. 'Ah, I don't care,' said Spencer with a shrug. 'I can go home and get on the golf course.' That was his attitude. Well, you would never hear Davis say that. Playing snooker and winning snooker matches was his life. He was a professional and took the game to a new level. Then Hendry came along and took it a stage further.

Someone once said to Jimmy, 'Wouldn't you like to have been more like Steve Davis?' Jimmy was stunned, almost offended by the question. 'Why would I like to be more like Steve Davis?' he asked. Those two were like chalk and cheese. Davis's idea of a good time would certainly be very different from Jimmy's. Whether Jimmy's approach to the game was completely formed out of Alex's is open to debate. I personally think it was. I think Jimmy based his game and his attitude to the game on Alex Higgins. It's as simple as that. He had that wild streak and he loved the excitement that Alex could create. He wanted to create some of that excitement himself. Davis? He just wanted to win. That's where the difference was between them as characters and players. He had made his debut in 1979 but lost in a match against Dennis Taylor.

The thing I remember about that match was that during one frame, while Taylor was at the table, Davis decided to eat a sandwich. He was inexperienced and not used to long matches. So during the proceedings he got terrible hunger pangs. Seems reasonable, doesn't it? But quite a lot of people in the players' room watching it on the television monitors thought it showed a total lack of respect for Dennis. I had never seen it done before and I have never seen it done since. I would say in his defence, though, that if you are hungry you are hungry. It's that simple.

When the 1990s came around Stephen Hendry had added a new aspect to the game. By this time Alex had become a bit of a caricature of himself. He had his reputation as a bit of a hellraiser, but, playing-wise, he was clearly on the decline. What I found sad was how people's behaviour towards him changed. People who had previously run around in circles for Alex suddenly didn't want to know him any longer. That was how fickle these people were. It repulsed me, to be honest. That's how quickly people can turn. They weren't true friends and they showed their true colours. Alex started getting more and more bitter with the game. He was feeling very hard done by with how he had been treated by the Snooker Association. As his career began to decline, they started to be even harder on him, because they no longer felt they needed him. Where they had previously been soft on him for the sake of the popularity of the game, they now began to take the gloves off. This made him increasingly bitter. Indeed, the authorities got tougher with everyone. Young players were quickly stamped on.

The game was changing fast. It is arguable that sometimes the authorities went too far the other way. Having perhaps felt they were too lax with Alex, they possibly went in too strongly on others in the aftermath. Some of the rules in the game now are a little bit over the top. I think the fine for players who concede a frame early is a shame. As I have said, when you make a mistake in snooker it is so frustrating when you then have to wait and wait for your chance to put it right. So that rule seems a shame. The fines are handed out too readily as well. It seems to me that most of the players in the game are currently getting fines for something or other. They can be more relaxed at times, I think. Ronnie O'Sullivan has sometimes been treated softer than he might have been.

Alex was often at loggerheads with other people in the game of snooker, but he always had celebrity friends. He became friendly with Oliver Reed and they went on some legendary sessions together. Reed had been fascinated by Alex as he rose in the game. He had arranged for them to meet at his home and they quickly hit it off. There was always a classic story every time they met, like the time Reed successfully dared Alex to drink perfume. Then, one morning, they woke up after a solid night of drinking. Alex had a fearful hangover and Reed said he had the solution. 'Here,' he said passing Alex a glass filled with a strange-looking liquid. 'Drink that, that'll sort you right out.' It was a combination of liqueur and washing-up liquid, but Alex had knocked the whole lot back in one before he realised he had been pranked. As an observer said, Alex was burping bubbles and farting perfume.

CHAPTER 7

MIMICRY AND COMMENTARY

Soon it was time for me to take a step towards celebrity myself. The game of snooker originally had just one commentator — that was Ted Lowe, of course. But then, as the BBC started to show more snooker, they would add an ex-professional as a summariser. When you're playing, though, you never even think about that. In my case, I was always known for doing impersonations of people. It's actually a sign of the times that there were so many different characters in sport, with different mannerism or technique. Nowadays they are all much more similar, but back then there were plentiful opportunities for mimicry. It started when we were doing a tournament at one of the holiday camps. This was another tournament that Alex hadn't been invited to because people were more and more fearful of him. On one particular evening they decided to have a charity night, in which six professionals would get up and do trick shots for the delight of the holidaymakers. I was the last on the bill to get up and by the time I did so there was not a single trick shot that had not already been done that evening. So I had to think fast.

I went to the table and decided to try to make people laugh. I seemed to have a way of doing this. Fortunately, one of the pieces of wood on the table fell off, so I made a quip about that and got the audience laughing and on my side. Next, I decided to do some impersonations of well-known snooker players. There was Spencer, who was always renowned for sniffing a lot, and Reardon, who was always laughing with the crowd. Then there was my impersonation of Alex, which was the simplest of the lot. He was always rushing round the table, pulling faces and twitching. It went down really well and people advised me to do more of it. Then, in the mid-1980s, a semi-final finished early at the Crucible, so I did impersonations of other snooker players again, to please the crowd. David Vine, who was the frontman for the BBC, came up and said, 'You've just got 25 grand of free publicity there, you know.' He explained that my act had gone down so well that there would soon follow requests for me to appear at clubs and other entertainment centres. There were only a few proper snooker tournaments at the time, so I needed all the money I could get.

Fortunately, he was right, and the work was soon flooding in. He was a bit out on the figures, though: it was more like a million that it brought in.

Mind you, I landed myself in hot water, too. Someone once asked me if I had any new impersonations to do. I explained that the problem was that Steve Davis had become so successful that all the other players at that time were copying his style and mannerisms in the hope of becoming successful themselves. 'So the problem is that if I do an impersonation of Steve Davis I would also be doing an impersonation of 90 per cent of players around,' I explained. The press managed to spin this quote into a sensational headline: JOHN VIRGO SAYS STEVE DAVIS IS RUINING SNOOKER. Luckily, Steve knew I had been spun.

The impersonations were successful and quickly I was being asked to be on 'standby' for any tournament session that looked as if it might finish prematurely. So I was becoming more of an entertainer at the time. I was once referred to as 'the Lee Trevino of snooker', in reference to the humorous golfer. I never saw myself as that, personally. It does rebound on you to a degree, though. I once got handed a letter of complaint that had been sent to the BBC. It came from a teacher who taught special-needs children and she wrote that, when I did the Alex Higgins impersonation, I was 'mocking every disabled child in the country'. I was devastated. All I had done was impersonate Alex's funny way of walking round the table and here I was being accused of mocking unfortunate children. It felt very unfair indeed. The producer who handed me the letter was on my side. He took it back and tore it up. 'Some people, eh?' he said. It was just a bit of entertainment and humour; I wasn't taking the mickey out of anyone apart from Alex. I should have reported that teacher to the education authorities.

This was the first thing that moved me towards commentary. The other factor that helped me a lot was my place on the board. With many changes going on in the game, the BBC were keen to keep in with the board. Nick Hunter, the executive producer, was keen to keep the association going and he suddenly asked me if I fancied trying a bit of commentary. I was surprised. Someone from Salford commentating on the BBC? I thought the BBC was all about posh Southern voices. People tell me it's changed and I reply, 'Well if I ever hear someone from Wolverhampton reading the ten o'clock news then I'll agree with you.' Anyway, they gave me a three-day trial period.

I remember those early days of commentary well. The commentator Jack Karnehm told me when he was chairman of the Billiard and Snooker Control Council (BSCC) that he hated snooker. He had a big reputation as a commentator but I knew that he hated the game. He told me how the commentary should work between us and how we would divide the duties. I was trying to not say too much, which was a big directive from the BBC at the time. It has since become more American in style. They actively want to hear the commentators talk a lot, but back then they wanted us more quiet.

On the second day of my commentary trial the executive producer approached me and asked me how I was finding it. 'It's all right, I quite like it,' I replied. He said, 'I think you're doing very well but we've already got one Ted Lowe.' Unbeknown to me, I was commentating like Ted Lowe. I was whispering just as he did! I soon put that right and started to develop my own style. And soon I was actually commentating alongside Ted. On one particular day while we were commentating on a tournament in Dubai, there was a small period of silence between us, which I didn't think was a problem because when we had worked for the BBC we had always been told that they didn't want us to talk too much. However, on this day, as the silence continued for a short while, suddenly the American director's irate voice came through our earphones. 'Have the commentators died? What's going on in there? Speak – that's what you're being paid for!' That was when I first realised that the commentary world was beginning to change. I continued to develop my style and I tried to bring to the commentary box the sort of conversation that professional players would be having as they watched a game themselves. Ted, on the other hand, would tell the viewers where the player lived, who he was married to and how many children he had.

Of course I made the odd mistake just as any commentator did, and I occasionally found myself in *Private Eye*'s infamous 'Colemanballs' column. One time they asked me to record a summary of how Alex won the 1982 World Championship. The text concluded: 'And to think none of this might have happened, had it not been for that unbelievable 69.' It was hard to say that with a straight face and voice. I have enjoyed commentating, though, and in the main people have been very positive in their feedback. Occasionally, people say I have been too excitable, but that's me. I love the game of snooker. The same applies to Alex. When you are really passionate about something, you can do things that are odd and exceptional, and can even seem a bit over the top to a less passionate soul. But I do get passionate, and, if it's a good match, I want to take every ounce of my own excitement and give that to the audience. It's about sharing the passion. I hope it works and I believe it does. I want everyone to enjoy it as much as possible.

When we did *Big Break* Jim Davidson asked me, 'Do you never get nervous?' I never did, though. All I was doing on the show was standing and talking about a game that I knew everything about. The same applied to match commentary. There wasn't really much to be nervous about. To me, it was a blissful job to have. I was soon looking beyond playing and instead to television work. It is a hard realisation when the ability at the table declines. Snooker is a hard game when you've made a mistake. You have that double frustration that not only have you missed an absolute sitter but you then have to sit there and watch the other guy clear up. You don't have that immediate opportunity to atone for your mistake as you do in many other sports. You sit there devastated and seething. There's nothing you can do until your opponent lets you back in.

As my game began to decline I was worried. I thought, What are you going to do now? There are only so many impersonations you can do! I was almost back in front of that boss at the office, who told me I would end up selling shoelaces in the park. I wasn't at that time a natural at the after-dinner circuit, though I did do them. Then came the phone call asking me if I wanted to do a BBC quiz show. The pilot had been recorded with the late Mike Reid and the snooker referee Len Ganley, but the chemistry wasn't right. Jim Davidson had just lost his job at Thames Television and I was coming to the end of my career, so it all just fell into place for us. We had a big break thanks to *Big Break*. We worked well because my natural demeanour can be quite deadpan. He was a comedian and I was more sombre. Likewise, he was a southern Conservative; I was the Salford socialist. It all just worked.

That said, there was a painful moment for me as the critics turned their pens to the first episode. The first one

147

had been shown on the second Tuesday of the World Championship. Having lost in the first round, I was now in the commentary box. The Wednesday morning, after the first showing, I went into the Embassy Room for a coffee. The first person I saw was Jack Karnehm, who informed me that there had been a write-up of the show. I found the newspaper and prepared to read the verdict. I felt sure that my experience as chairman had sufficiently thickened my skin to anything. It did hurt, though. The *Yorkshire Post*'s television critic Alison Graham wrote, 'The combination of Jim Davidson and snooker triggers the sort of cerebral meltdown previously achieved only by *Are You Being Served?*.' So far, so bad. Turning to my performance, she said I had 'the self-assurance of Frankie Howerd trying to split the atom'. She concluded that *Big Break* was 'The nadir of non-achievement – anyone who watched without weeping deserved a Purple Heart.'

Well, if that wasn't a writer desperately trying to make a name for herself, I don't know what is. Not that the criticism stopped there. Alexander Clyde, a columnist for the London *Evening Standard* – and importantly to me also a writer for the *Pot Black* snooker magazine – described our show as 'the worst thing that had ever happened to snooker'. He added that the show should be taken off air immediately.

Fortunately, the viewers disagreed with Graham and Clyde. When Saatchi and Saatchi had advised us snooker players to go on a media training course, I refused. My policy was that if someone asks me a question I would aim to give an honest answer. I was only to learn later that, sadly, that is not always the best policy.

I've often thought I should have stayed just being a snooker player rather than getting involved in the game's politics. But I would guess that being on the board helped me to move onto commentating and I always enjoyed the fun aspects around the game like doing my impersonations. Alex was once on the phone to his then wife Lynn when he saw me on a television screen in the background doing my impersonation of him. 'Quick, Lynn,' he said, encouraging her to switch on, 'JV's doing me on TV.' He then burst out laughing. Indeed, one time at an exhibition match I did a series of impressions that night, culminating in the one of Alex. That was always an easy one to do. Ray Reardon was there and he was pretended to be annoyed that I didn't do the impersonation of him. 'You've not done one of me,' he complained.

'Well, I didn't want to offend you, Ray,' I replied. He then demanded I do it.

'We want to see it, don't we?' he said, turning to the audience. People tended to have more of a sense of humour towards themselves than you might think. I remember I had a joke about Steve Davis that was quite cutting. It involved my reading a book about the origin of names. The punchline was that under 'Davis' it said

'Intelligent, charming and witty,' but under Steve it had 'Not very'. Steve got wind of this joke and told me he thought it was hilarious.

CHAPTER 8

MAN BEHAVING BADLY

I don't think that any of us who knew Alex expected him to live to a ripe old age. His lifestyle was such that it never seemed likely. I honestly believe that he lived for the adulation that he got at the peak of his game. He craved it. It was around the late 1970s that he was getting in more and more trouble. We were getting complaints the whole time at the board. They were not always for serious matters, but, once we began to get three or four every meeting, we began to get concerned. To us, he looked be on a downward spiral. On reflection, I think my winning the UK championship in 1979 gave him a kick up the pants that ultimately spurred him on to the 1982 World Championship win. Even that year he was not at his peak, but neither was Reardon, a fact that helped Alex win.

I didn't feel that Alex was in control of his life at this stage. His life to me was snooker, going out and creating a frenzy among the public. Near the end of his life he became more and more outrageous. But then he could rein it in. When we had him on that first series of *Big Break* he was fine. He still had a sense of when to misbehave and when to behave. He was never completely outrageous. He had an 'off button', you could say. He was invited to play in a pro–celebrity golf tournament. Among those taking part was Sean Connery and he was very polite to him. He was partnering Greg Norman on the course. Now Alex was not the greatest golf player in the world. He wasn't bad, but not the best. Norman was trying to offer him a bit of advice on how to improve. After Alex hit one particularly bad shot, Norman's caddy came up and said, 'Don't worry, we all have a bad day.' Alex replied, 'Well if that cunt wasn't always telling me what to do things would have been better.' Norman hadn't heard this, as he was not in earshot at the time, but the caddy for some reason went over and told him.

Lo and behold, the next thing we know Norman is reluctant to play on until Alex gives him a proper apology. So the game nearly came to an immediate end. The point is, though, that in the hotel Alex had been almost fawningly polite to Sean Connery. It was all 'Mr Connery' this and 'Mr Connery' that. So, you see, he really could pick and choose when he was rude and when he was not just polite but almost deferential. He could be as nice as ninepence when he wanted to. A guaranteed way to get him to explode was to walk up to him and eulogise to him about what a great player he was. Oh, he could really erupt when people did that. I lost count of the number of times people came up to him with generous praise only for him to tell them to 'Fuck off'. Then he'd storm off leaving them red-faced and open-mouthed. All they had done was tell him how great he was! He saw it as a sign of weakness.

I will never forget when we were in a bar once and this fellow came over to us and said, 'Let me down last week, you did,' as an opening gambit to Alex.

'Why? What did I do?' asked Alex, a bit bemused.

'I bet a thousand pounds on you in that tournament last week and I lost the lot because of you. That's the last time I have a bet on you, I can tell you.' I was fascinated to see what Alex's response would be. As usual, he managed to surprise everyone.

'Oh, you're a big gambler then are you?' he asked the man.

'Yeah, I love a gamble,' the man replied.

Then Alex took a 10p coin out of his pocket, flicked it in the air and covered it as it landed on his hand. 'Heads or tails – for a thousand pounds?' he asked the fella. 'Go on, you're the one who says you're a big gambler.' The fella quickly backed down. 'No, I'm not having that,' he said.

'Oh,' said Alex, 'I thought you said you were the big gambler!'

There was another time when we were in Potters. There

was a new nine-ball pool table there and Bill Werbeniuk was saying that he had played a lot of pool. I told him that I had never been so keen on pool. With the size of the pockets and other aspects of it, I didn't really see the skill, I explained. Alex was sitting there quietly listening to us. His eyebrows shot up when Bill said, 'There isn't a snooker player in the world who would beat me in a game of pool. None of them would want to play me for money.' Alex leant over and counted out £3,000 onto the bar in £50 notes. He said, 'Come on, then. I'll play you for that now.' Bill was stunned and tried to back out. 'No, come on,' insisted Alex. 'I'll play you for £3,000 now.' Bill said he didn't have £3,000 on him. 'No problem, you can give my boss an IOU. Come on now, me and you!' Bill wouldn't play him, but that was just typical of Alex – he was as brave as a lion.

Then there was the very sad side of this. A guy rang me up because he was trying to put on an exhibition match at a leisure centre in Norwich. Jimmy suggested he book Alex. At this point Alex had recently retired and he was struggling financially due to all the money he had gambled away. Jimmy was a good friend and he would try to get work for Alex when he could. He would do the same for me. That's the sort of nice guy Jimmy is. The promoter was all for the idea of Alex being involved – he may have retired but he was still great for the box office. The place was packed on the first night and Alex wasn't having a good game. He got increasingly tetchy and started complaining about this and that. 'Move away, you're breathing too loudly,' he snapped at the referee. Halfway through the evening the promoter realised that he neither needed nor wanted Alex's continued involvement in the event. Alex was proving more trouble than he was worth, so the promoter had a quiet word with Jimmy, explaining that he didn't want Alex to come back the following evening.

Jimmy explained to me what had been said and asked me what I thought. The socialist in me kicked in and I said that we had to stand by our friend. I said that if he didn't want Alex back the following night then *I* didn't intend to return the following night. Call it 'union' or whatever you like, that was how I saw it. Jimmy said he felt exactly the same. After the first night was over we went out for a meal at a Chinese restaurant. The promoter was there and he was chatting away happily to Jimmy and me, but ignoring Alex. I watched this dark cloud gather over Alex. He could sense what was going on and he started to pick on the promoter.

Now it's worth stating at this stage that this promoter guy was a big tough man. He could have been a heavyweight boxer. Alex didn't let that stop him, though. 'You see you, you couldn't organise a piss-up in a brewery,' he sneered across the table. 'That table you had us playing on tonight was fucking crap.' This fella could have easily knocked Alex out but that didn't stop him in his tirade. It worked. He was invited back the next night and he played much better. But he had stood up well for himself and shown again how brave he could be. He never knew officially that the promoter was thinking of removing him from the event. Had he done so I've no doubt he would have physically attacked him. Seriously, he could be like a little fearless terrier when he wanted to.

We were already seeing a turning-point in attitudes to him, though. In his heyday there had always been people ready and willing to make an excuse for him when he behaved badly. He could get away with things because there was this aura around him that made people forgive him his excesses. But now the tide was turning, and the slightest thing he did came to be less easy to forgive. People were deciding that he was more trouble than he was worth. Their patience threshold was being lowered and previous so-called friends and allies were deserting him. In the last four years or so of his life, I felt Alex owed a lot to Jimmy, who was always loyal to him. They were always in touch and Jimmy was always trying to get him onto the bill of exhibition matches. One time when he was too ill to take part himself, Jimmy suggested Alex as a replacement. The promoter had worked with Alex before and Alex had always insisted he have a bit of his joint when he smoked one. The poor fella never wanted any. But that was how Alex was: he had that childlike quality of wanting to share things.

Anyway, Alex was lined up as Jimmy's replacement. I was taking part in this tournament too and when I arrived the promoter came straight up to me. 'We've got a problem,' he said. 'Jimmy can't make it and his replacement is supposed to be Alex Higgins.' I said I knew all this and asked exactly what the problem was. 'Well,' said the promoter, 'Dennis Taylor says he doesn't take part in tournaments including Alex Higgins.' The legacy of Alex threatening to have Dennis shot after a row during a tournament was still living on (and I'll tell you more about that in Chapter 13). I went to the dressing room to see if I could sort this out. 'I've told people that I will never play snooker with Alex Higgins,' declared Dennis. He was in no mood to compromise. Alex, meanwhile, was in another dressing room, unaware of the drama erupting. Eventually we did persuade Dennis and he reluctantly agreed to play. Jimmy had once again sorted Alex out with a gig. Not that Jimmy was immune to fallings-out with Alex. Nobody was. Alex didn't see it that Jimmy was doing him a favour getting him all these tournaments. On the contrary, Alex thought he was doing Jimmy a favour by agreeing to grace them with his presence. That was his mentality.

There were so many times I clashed with him. Everyone who knew him did. I owed him £180 and I kept asking his manager when I was going to see Alex next, so I could pay him back. Then, on St Leger Day, Shergar was favourite for the race. We knew Shergar's work rider – the person who would take the horse early in the morning for an exercise gallop. Alex rang me up and said, 'You owe me £180.' I said I was aware of this and that I had been trying to pay him back. He then asked me what the chances were of Shergar in the St Leger. I said Shergar was well fancied. 'OK,' he said, 'put me £1,000 on Shergar.' I reminded him that I owed him only £180. 'Well, you know, put it on and if it gets beat I will owe you.' I said this wasn't an option, but that I was willing to put the £180 on for him. 'Oh, fuck you,' he stormed. 'I'll have £180 on it, then.' I knew that if I had put a £1,000 bet on for him it would have taken me years to get it back if Shergar didn't win – which it didn't. I was refusing to go along with that. You had to draw the line that way sometimes.

CHAPTER 9

FAME AMONG THE FAMOUS

As we saw in Chapter 5, people often compared Alex to that other sporting great of Belfast, the football legend George Best. I never saw them as the same. But when Alex was ill he said he wanted a bigger funeral than George Best, so there was a rivalry there for sure. That said, I don't believe that anyone other than Alex himself thought he was bigger than George. He certainly thought that but I doubt anyone else did. George was the biggest thing to come out of Belfast. He had the women, the fame – everything. Indeed, if there was a choice of going out socially with either Alex or George I would rather go with George. I just felt with George it was a more predictable experience. You could talk about football and whatever you wanted. You had a laugh, whereas with Alex you wouldn't know what would happen. All of a sudden he would catch the eye of someone he felt was looking at him funny and then all hell would break loose. You could be stuck in the middle of that as an innocent bystander. With George you were more likely to be just having a laugh, a drink and a chat.

Here's an example of what George was like. There was a television panel show called *Sport in Question* on HTV. It was not unlike *Question Time*, but focused on sports rather than politics, and was not quite so grandiose. Henry Kelly was the anchorman. I was on one night with various guests, including Tommy Docherty. At the end of the show, Kelly said, 'Well that's all for this week. I'd like to thank our panel. On next week's show we have George Best...' Docherty then interrupted and said, 'There's as much chance of him turning up as there is Lord Lucan!' A few days later I was in a nightclub in London. At this particular club, when you walked in the owner would put a bottle of champagne on the bar if he liked you. So, as you can imagine, George went in there a lot. This particular night I saw him in there. I told him what Docherty had said about him on *Sport in Question*. He said, 'I'll tell you what, just to show Tommy, I'm going to make sure I'm bloody well there.' He was absolutely determined to prove Tommy Docherty wrong. Anyway, I saw Henry Kelly a month later and I asked him how it went with George. 'Oh, he never turned up,' shrugged Henry.

So he wasn't the most reliable character but you still felt more at ease with him than you did with Alex. Girls used to throw themselves at him in nightclubs and, though Alex was not often short of a bit of female attention, they never threw themselves at him to the same degree that they did with George. Not that I can talk: they were probably actively throwing themselves *away* from *me*! But George had that magnetism. He was on a different level from Alex. Also, remember, he played a team game and that gave him a different character from Alex, who played an individual game of course. He created a more dangerous atmosphere than George because he revelled in being out. That said, one time I had an uncomfortable liaison involving George, myself and a policeman. Well, kind of...

I got invited to do a lot of pantomimes. The actors would be up in arms when Australian soap stars and reality-television stars turned up and took their places on stage. I received a few snotty reviews in local newspapers – but I didn't care. I loved being out there, performing on stage. One year I was playing the part of a Chinese policeman at the Ashcroft Theatre in Croydon. This was my third year doing pantomime. In the neighbouring theatre, George Best was doing an 'evening with' slot with Alan Mullery. I didn't join my play until 20 minutes in, so I could afford to be fairly laid back about preparations. I didn't even start to get ready until 10 minutes after the 'half-hour' call. I had to put a bit of rouge on my cheeks and some eyeliner. Then I'd don the suit, which was a comedic Chinese policeman outfit. I was sitting there in the dressing room, all done up and just waiting for my slot.

Then there was a knock on the door. An usher said, 'A message from George Best: he's in the green room and wondered if you wanted a drink before you went on.' I thought this sounded like a great idea. 'Yeah, tell him I'll be right down,' I said. Then I turned round and caught sight of myself in the mirror. I jumped with shock – I had totally forgotten I was dressed up in character. I couldn't let George down. He was not just a friend but one of my big heroes. Nor did I have time to change out of my costume. So I realised I had no choice but to go and meet George Best for a drink, dressed up as a comedy Chinese policeman! I felt a little self-conscious and silly to say the least, so to try to bring some levity to the moment I did a kind of Charlie Chaplin walk as I went into the room.

He said, 'John! What's happened?'

I replied, 'Steve Davis took all the money, George!'

He liked that. We had a laugh and a drink.

As I have said, a famous man who did enjoy Alex's company was the legendary Oliver Reed. Still, perhaps that overstates their bond. I wouldn't necessarily go as far as describing them as friends. It was probably closer to being the case that Reed tolerated Alex. It is true, though, that Alex captured his imagination. He captured lots of people's imagination. The way he played was so different that it was like a turn-on. People loved seeing him play. This was true of nobody more than creative people. They loved him because, I believe, they could appreciate that there was almost an artistry to Alex's game. They appreciated the difference more than anyone. The actor John Hurt loved Alex, too. The broadcaster, writer and wit Stephen Fry is a big snooker fan and he would say that it was Alex who first got him watching the game, even if Steve Davis is his favourite now.

Here's a great story to illustrate how famous creative types loved him. I always found it funny the time that Alex was playing Dennis Taylor in the final of the Masters. He was far in front but then got beaten in the final frame. A few days later the film critic Barry Norman was interviewing the actor Paul Newman. He asked Newman how he and his wife Joanne Woodward were enjoying their stay in London. Newman said, 'Well, what an amazing night we had on Sunday night. Me and Joanne were watching the final of the snooker, between that Hurricane Higgins and that Dennis Turner. We were in the hotel and Joanne was jumping up and down on the bed watching it. We were so excited by Hurricane Higgins!' This shows the impact he had, but note also that he got Dennis's name wrong, not Alex's.

He hooked up with Marianne Faithfull once. Backstage, at a match I was playing him in, he had her with him. I went to his dressing room in the interval and he said, 'JV, this is

Marianne — Marianne Faithfull. You've probably heard of her.' She wasn't at all like I would have imagined. I didn't realise until that moment that she was Irish, for starters. In the second half she was so drunk that she wanted to sit in the aisle on the stairs, rather than in the seats. The security men moved her. She argued with them and they ended up ejecting her. Naturally, this became a newspaper story. MARIANNE FAITHFULL IN RUMPUS AT SNOOKER SHOWDOWN, etc. They quoted her and she said, 'I only went along to see my friend, Alex. I don't know who the other man was.' Ouch. How fucking typical, I thought. I had a bit of a twinge, I must admit. But nothing I couldn't overcome.

Another time Peter O'Toole wanted to meet me — but guess who it was who he wanted to talk about. It turned out he was a big fan of mine, which was nice. He had guessed, just from my commentary, that I enjoyed a bet. Now, I had been warned about him. I was told when he was drunk he was 'worse than Higgins' — and that's quite a plaudit. He turned up late, drank water all night and all he did was ask me about other snooker players. Naturally, O'Toole, who was a bit of a hellraiser himself, was interested in Alex.

When you get famous, you find that famous people are more willing to speak to you. I had a sniff of that when I was presenting *Big Break*. I did have some amusing experiences as well. Brian Blackburn wrote a script for the show that would see me walk on at the beginning dressed in a leotard with two girls from the sports entertainment show *Gladiators* at each side of me. We then did a sketch that involved my being called not Wolf, like the famous male star of *Gladiators*, but Rottweiler. Sometime later I was playing in a celebrity golf match and Frankie Vaughan came up to me and said, 'I must say, John, I love that show that you and Jim are doing. But that one that was on last week, when you came on like a Gladiator – you've got bigger tits than my wife!'

Alex liked his music. He was a cultured, intelligent man with an artistic side to him. I've seen him add funny little pictures to an autograph. He could do the *Times* crossword; he was as bright as a button. But, of course, his niche in life became playing snooker, and he played that with real panache. Away from the game he was always entertaining – not always in the most positive of ways. He was once having an argument with his girlfriend in a hotel. The television was the first thing to go through the window; soon afterwards, out flew Alex. He landed on his ankle and broke it. His ankle was in a cast and he was expected to miss lots of tournaments. I think he missed only one though. In those he played he hopped around the table. Such tenacity. Soon after this we played a tournament in which there were four tables, each in a separate cubicle. But you could just see into each cubicle from its neighbouring one. I knew when Alex was playing because I could see his head bobbing up and down as he was hopping round the table.

It can be hard to keep healthy romantic relationships going when you are a professional sportsman. Athletes from many sports, from golf to snooker, have this dilemma: they are either doing well and therefore in many tournaments and away from home a lot of the time, or they are not doing well and therefore are stuck at home in a tense atmosphere because they are not bringing the money in for the household. I would sometimes come home from practising to be quizzed by my then-wife. She would ask how it went and I would explain that I was playing out of my skin. But then, when I went on to the next tournament and got beaten, I'd go home and have to explain why I could turn on the skill in practice but not in the real thing. Your partner ends up asking why they haven't got the big house that comes from consistent success. I could tell my family that I was better than Steve Davis when he first appeared, but the record books will tell the different story. You can't go in the face of facts, though. If you're not getting the right results, the money isn't coming in. Then you are not able to provide the sort of lifestyle that people expect. I think that mentality then seeped over to me and I was going into tournaments in the wrong frame of mind. It comes at you from all sides when you are not getting the results. People start to turn their backs on you.

Imagine how it must have been for Alex. It must have been a thousand times worse, especially during that 10-year drought he had. I've spoken to actors who have had a similar experience. They see the other actors swanning round in limousines and staying in hotel suites, but they cannot get the work themselves. It can be very tough and those around you can find it just as hard. It can creep up on you, this problem with fame and celebrity. People expect things of you that you mostly cannot deliver. That can be a very hard pill to swallow if you are not at the top. That certainly caused rifts in my marriage, so I've little doubt that there were rifts caused in Alex's marriage.

When it came to the game itself Alex's relationship with Ray Reardon was possibly the most interesting to witness. Reardon was originally a miner in Tredegar, a mining community in Monmouthshire. He became a miner at just 14 but after several years of that he suffered an accident and quit to become a police officer. So he had quite a tough life prior to snooker. I always remember when I asked him what it was like down the mines. 'Let me put it this way, John,' he said. 'If anyone asks you to go down and get them some coal, tell them to go down and get it themselves.'

Reardon beat Spencer in the English Amateur Final. I always felt with Spencer – and this was something I felt about a lot of players, including Alex – that he never reproduced in tournaments the sort of form he showed practising. The man who could do it was Reardon. This was because he didn't play fancy screw shots and the like. He was a superb single-ball potter. Steve Davis might have been better in a safety exchange, but Reardon was a masterful player. He had a great art of long shots, which are known as 'shots for nothing'. This made him a formidable opponent. On long shots, if they didn't go in, he hadn't lost anything, but if they did go in then it was game on for Reardon.

I once said to Mark Williams, the new kid on the block, that he reminded me of Reardon. He looked at me as if to query whether or not it was meant as a compliment – but it *was* a compliment. He was the archetypal match player. He had the complete game and the psychology. When he played Alex in a big final he knew he could tempt him into playing unwise shots. He dangled little carrots out for Alex to try. Over a long match he knew that he would profit from these carrots and that he would wear him down.

That said, Reardon's record against Spencer was not so strong. Spencer had more of an all-round game. I would have thought that Reardon probably really enjoyed playing Alex. Percentage wise he knew that he could really freeze Alex out and wear him down with his tactics. So you knew that you could really do well against him and it was probably a lot of fun for Reardon. He was a hard, hard man as a result of his life as a young miner and then a policeman, and that came out in his game at the top level. He was a real tough opponent.

Reardon played all the holiday camps in Devon. We were drawn in the same group in a professional tournament and Reardon suggested a deal whereby whichever of us lost would be the one to do the holiday camps. He wanted to play a bit of golf and didn't fancy doing the camps. I won and so I progressed in the tournament while he went home. During a chat with Reardon's wife, I asked how he coped with defeat when he got home. She replied, 'Well, this is the first time I've known him to return home from a defeat without kicking the cat up the arse.' Reardon was a tactician. People say that you should 'play your own game', but I think when he came up against Alex he wasn't thinking of playing his own game. He was analysing how he could tailor his game to beat Alex. They used to say that snooker was like a game of chess but I think recently, particularly since Stephen Hendry came into the game, it is more like a game of pool. You come in, pot a red, pot the black, try to smash the reds open. Reardon wouldn't play like that at all. He knocked only a few reds out at a time, so if he made a mistake he wasn't leaving it open for his opponent.

Now it's more of an attacking game. Alex would fit in the modern-day game much better than Reardon. Thorburn and Griffiths, too, were players who slowed down and closed down the game. Alex would calm his nerves with a few stiff drinks, whereas Griffiths would calm his with a nice deep-breathing exercise and a slow approach to the game. He didn't want it ever to be said that he missed a shot because he rushed it. Alex? There aren't enough fingers on your hands to count the number of times he fluffed a shot because he had rushed it. No matter what anyone tells you about snooker, if you cannot pot long balls, you are not going to win many games. Spencer took some risks but he too was a good long-ball potter, which is why he did quite well against Reardon.

When we were brought up and we first heard about snooker, we'd watch it on *Grandstand* in the late 1950s and early 1960s. There were week-long matches in Leicester Square Hall, London. People from the theatre on their afternoons off would pop down there to watch. The audience was peppered with actors and actresses. There was something genteel about watching it and hearing the click of the snooker balls.

There was always a feeling at that stage that the players were sometimes giving each other a chance, partly to stretch out the professional games. Reardon took that competitive nature that existed in the amateur game and brought that mentality into the professional game. He really shook it up for the better. Nowadays when I hear about games being thrown or other corruptions, I think back to the game of snooker before Reardon emerged, and that was not a game you wanted to bet on. It was like wrestling – you just couldn't help suspecting that some of it was fixed. How can anyone watch a game like that? I think my reason for enjoying a sport is that I would want to have a bet on it. So, if there is the slightest whiff of anything dodgy, I am not interested.

Reardon and Alex gave snooker that competitive edge it needed to make it more exciting. People started coming through the door and starting betting on it. Spencer was the same. Reardon more than anyone was the one who brought that hard-edged competitive side to the game. It's no coincidence that when Ronnie O'Sullivan's form suffered his dad sent him to Reardon for a bit of coaching. Typical of Ray: Ronnie had his hair gelled and so did Ray, even in his 70s! In any case, I think he was key in Ronnie's resurgence.

There's a lovely story that highlights Reardon's nature. He was playing a game of golf at a Torquay club one day and he saw a ball on a fairway that he knew wasn't his. He realised that someone must have hit a ball over onto his fairway. This fella came over to him and said, 'You're Ray Reardon – six times world snooker champion. Can you answer me one question – what's the main difference between snooker and golf?' Reardon fixed his eyes on him and said, 'Well, I've been playing snooker for 55 years and I've never lost a ball.' He then walked off. That is what he's like – a great sense of humour. He was his own man. Dennis Taylor tells a story about Reardon in the dressing room after an exhibition match. A man came in and said, 'The Lord Mayor's downstairs and there's a bit of a buffet reception going on. Would you like to come down and meet him?' Ray looked at his watch and said, 'Nah, too late. I'm going to drive home.' He was reminded that it was the Lord Mayor, but he wouldn't budge. 'So what shall I tell the Lord Mayor?' asked the man, exasperated. 'Erm,' said Ray, 'tell him to fuck off!' That was Ray for you!

Players look for a new direction when they have stopped playing, including coaching sometimes. Alex had a lot of talent and he could have passed it on as a coach in theory, but that wasn't something that many of the professionals have ever been tempted to do. In the main, I think most of us learned by watching other players play. Nowadays you can buy a 'how-to' DVD or book for any sport under the sun. All the top players did 'how-to' books, which became almost a compulsory thing for any top star to do. If you have a natural ability and you watch top players closely you will pick up their techniques. You do need a love of the game as well, though. For all the tantrums Alex threw, he loved the game. If you love a game you will practise hard, and I think if you keep practising at anything you become better.

Terry Griffiths has made a career as a coach, but that's a rarity. He thinks you need certain beliefs and breathing patterns, so maybe there is something in that. But you do need that love. I love it, have done since the start. When I was working in that office it was always on my mind. Indeed, during pretty much every waking minute I would be thinking, I can't wait to get to that snooker club, I can't wait. I wanted to get the cue in my hand and start potting a few balls. There is a sinister flipside to this. When you get to the end of your career and your ability dries up and you stop being able to pot so many balls, that love can turn to a sort of hate. You just don't want to go out there any more. It's a dark time.

Could Alex have become a coach after his playing declined? James Wattana's manager felt he was lacking something and asked Spencer to help teach Wattana. Apparently, during one particular tournament when Wattana was struggling, Spencer went into his dressing room for a chat. Now, keep in mind that Wattana doesn't speak a lot of English, anyway, and apparently Spencer raised his voice at him. It was a real hairdryer moment. Wattana left the venue and went back to his hotel more confused than anything. Spencer realised that he might have overdone it and rang Wattana to apologise – at 3 am! Whether Alex could have done it and *how* he would have done it is open to question. He was not exactly a textbook player. I think often it is those who have not been so good at a sport who are better at analysing what goes into it. Often, those who excel at anything are wary of understanding the magic, for fear of losing it. I've done a bit of one-off coaching but I tell you: you need a lot of patience to do it.

CHAPTER 10

THE
ENTERTAINER

There were many good things to say about Alex's game, but perhaps the main was his eye on entertainment value. That is how he led. The game became popular after Alex's emergence, because people suddenly saw some money in it. Looking back now, I have no doubt that the best player I ever saw in terms of entertainment was Alex Higgins. Based on the record book and the way he went about the game, Stephen Hendry was probably the best. But in terms of sheer spectacle, in terms of a player who would get me out of my house and whom I would drive 50 miles to watch play live, that man was Alex Higgins. He was an absolute icon. He lived by the ethos of never, ever forgetting the spectators – he was an entertainer.

I had a similar view of the game in that regard. I think if

a sport is a professional sport, you must always remember the punters, the men and women coming through the turnstile. At one point the live audience in the arena had the option of hearing my television commentary through earpieces. The players would sometimes ask the authorities to turn the volume down, because they could hear my voice buzzing. During one game a ball had got lodged next to a pocket and both players were hitting safety shots. It was unbearably boring but eventually one of the players finally opened up the game. I said, 'We can breathe again folks!' and of course the audience – those who had not walked out due to boredom – fell about laughing.

One of the players, Peter Ebdon, made a complaint about the laughter, but the bigger principle at stake was that you have to remember the audience. Alex was a key figure in that – *the* key figure in the sport. Not that we should pretend he was the only one. Reardon liked a laugh with the audience if he missed a shot. Fred Davis was renowned for laughing and Dennis Taylor could get a reaction out of the audience. But Alex could entertain without making a joke. He just put people on the edges of their seats with the sheer drama of his game. He had a lonely life, much of it spent on trains travelling to tournaments, but he came alive at the table. Maybe that was why he was so good at crosswords. I wouldn't say he had that many very close friends, because he was forever travelling. All his family lived in Belfast.

I really admire the overseas players who have to live away

Above: Will he or won't he give the boy his autograph? *© Trevor Smith Photography*

Below: Alex the entertainer during his victorious 1982 final against Ray Reardon.

© Trevor Smith Photography

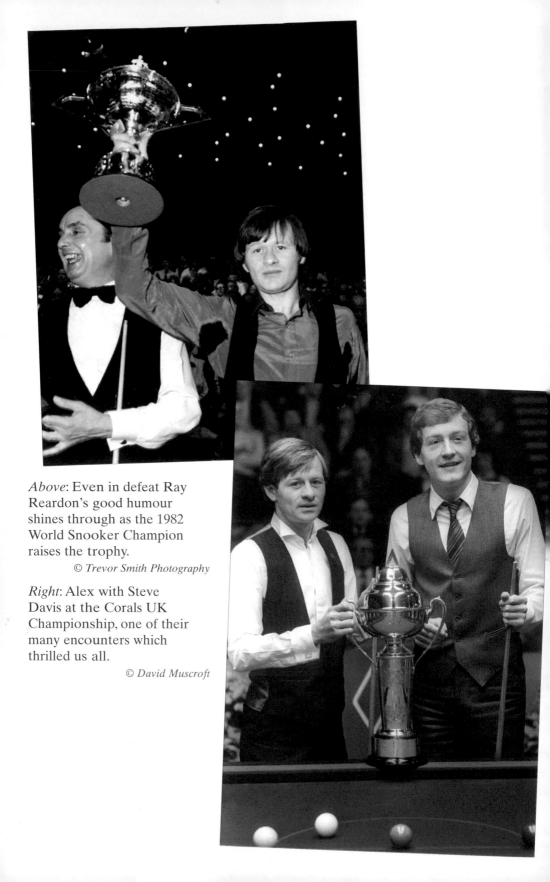

Above: Even in defeat Ray Reardon's good humour shines through as the 1982 World Snooker Champion raises the trophy.

© *Trevor Smith Photography*

Right: Alex with Steve Davis at the Corals UK Championship, one of their many encounters which thrilled us all.

© *David Muscroft*

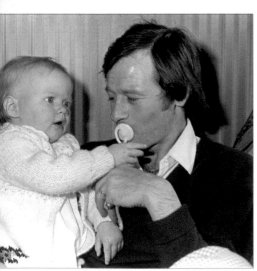

Above: Lynn and Lauren share the glory in 1982 as Peter Madden (left) looks on.

© Trevor Smith Photography

Bottom left: With Lauren at the disciplinary hearing after the 1982 championship.

© Trevor Smith Photography

Bottom right: Alex and I with Henry West (middle) and referees John Smyth and Peter Koniotes.

Above left: Shaking hands with Stephen Hendry with John Street refereeing at the 1999 Benson & Hedges Irish Masters final.   © *Eric Whitehead/Snookerimages*

Above right: They had a stormy relationship but there were friendlier times for Alex and Dennis Taylor.   © *David Muscroft*

Below: Fans celebrate as their hero wins the Masters – as ever, he gave his all.
© *Eric Whitehead/Snookerimages*

Above: World champions all. Nice of Alex to dress up!   © *Roger Lee Collection*

Below: The holy trinity: Alex flanked by Ronnie O'Sullivan and Jimmy White in 1998.

© *Eric Whitehead*

Above: Showing off the wound received jumping off a wall outside the Norbreck Castle Hotel in Blackpool in the early 1990s. Was he pushed or did he fall?

© *Eric Whitehead/Snookerimages*

Left: With girlfriend Siobhan Kidd in 1989 at the Benson & Hedges Irish Masters.

© *Eric Whitehead/Snookerimages*

Above: Alex holding court at a press conference in 1994.

© *Eric Whitehead/Snookerimages*

Left: Alex doing his Frank Sinatra impression while competing in 1994.

© *Trevor Smith Photography*

Alex's last-ever public appearance in spring 2010 at the Snooker Legends in Sheffield where he took on Jimmy White while I compered. © David Muscroft

from their families. Many of them spend months on end in hotels. But Alex lived a lonely and often insular life – maybe that was why he was so off the wall when he went out in public. When he was in London he sometimes stayed with Oliver Reed, but I don't think that did him so much good. There was not going to be much rest and recuperation when you're with Oliver Reed, is there?

Alex was an influential man. As he became more and more famous, I noticed that he sparked similar behaviour in others. I called these 'Higgins Moments' – and I was as susceptible to them as anyone. I was a bit of an angry young man, I suppose, but Alex had influenced me too. I think some of these moments were inspired by Alex. He seemed to let loose in me something that I didn't think was there. I found that there was a bit of a loose-cannon side to me, but I had never connected with it. Then, all of a sudden in Alex we've got a man behaving that way and getting away with it, but I saw that you didn't have to be a steady old snooker player. You could bring more passion and life to it. I've had some 'Higgins Moments' for sure.

I was still an amateur at the time. I'd watched all the games of the 1972 World Championship apart from the final. I was amazed by what I saw – inspirational stuff. All around the Northwest of England snooker was really beginning to take off. Every Sunday we went down to a snooker club and played challenge matches against the local players. It was a good afternoon out. However, I admit that I perhaps got a bit carried away with the Higgins thing. One day I missed an easy ball and in a moment of anger I mimed a spitting gesture, as if I had spat on the floor in disgust. I hadn't actually spat, but for one woman in the audience I had still overstepped the mark.

'Do you do that at home?' she cried.

My action was quite out of character – it was a pure Higgins moment. I quickly returned to normal and thought, Hang on, you can't behave like that!

There was another time when I missed an easy ball and responded with Higgins-esque petulance. I meant to swipe the balls across the table, thus symbolically conceding the frame. The trouble was, I swiped a bit too hard. The ball flew off the table straight into one of the bars. All I heard was the clattering of glasses as the ball smashed them to pieces. That was another Higgins moment.

I lost in the final of the Northern Area Amateur Championships. It was ironic because, just before I went there for the qualifiers, I had made a maximum break. My form was amazing, yet when I got there I couldn't pot a ball. I just froze completely. A couple of things upset me about that. The winner would have been invited to go to South Africa for the World Amateur Championships and I had got it into my head that if I won I was going to decline the invitation. I wanted to use that opportunity to make a real stand against apartheid. Unfortunately, because I didn't win, I never got invited and was unable to make that stand.

There was a snooker writer up in Newcastle, where we played and he had written, 'John Virgo is a good player but until he gets that chip off his shoulder he will never win anything.' So obviously this was the attitude I was portraying. Maybe it had always been lurking but it was almost as if Alex had given it permission to come out. I was now playing the game with a new attitude, influenced by Alex's example. I think we all imitate our heroes in many ways. I'm sure Jimmy White would say the same, that he was influenced by Alex. It was Alex who developed that faster style of play that so many have tried, and he made a success of it. He was very fast as he moved around the table, but he wasn't so fast on the shots themselves. So I got it all wrong when I tried to ape him. We still looked up to him though. He was like a breath of fresh air. We had watched Joe Davis and others on *Grandstand* but we never thought it would be a big spectator sport. Alex proved that it could be.

One close-run thing involved the Queen Mother. I came within a few inches of going a step further than a Higgins moment! I was at Sandown racecourse and it was Eclipse Day, which is the first Saturday in July. It is always a very busy day at Sandown. You get to see high-class thoroughbred horses. I was there trying to get a good view of the horses in the paddock but the crowd was four or five deep. All of a sudden somebody knocked me sideways. Luckily, because of the way I was standing and because I was surrounded by people I didn't fall over. But the knock had been hard enough to knock anyone off their feet in different circumstances. Instead, I sort of staggered to one side and in the split second after I had recovered my balance and I sort of swung out an arm. It was a natural response but at the last moment I realised that the Queen Mother was passing right by me, in the direction of my arm. She was there, little hat on her head, clutching her handbag. The knock into me had been one of her security men clearing a path for her, so she could get to the paddock. There was no 'Excuse me' or anything like that. Even when I think about it now I get a sort of shiver down my spine. I was within 12 inches of giving the Queen Mother a slap round the head.

Even Alex would have thought that was a bit much. He would probably have said, 'He's a bad loser, that Virgo – he'd probably backed a losing horse.' I wouldn't hit an old lady whoever she was, but if I had hit the Queen Mother that would have been my career over. This could have been the Higgins moment to end all Higgins moments.

Funnily enough I did have the 'bad loser' thing in common with Alex. Neither of us liked to lose, which of course some people say is a good trait for a sportsman to have. With Alex, though, it was as if you could almost see the black cloud descend over him. Anything could happen. I myself got the reputation as a bit of a troublemaker. I'm not blaming Alex for this, but I had changed from this steady player to someone who was very hyper round the table.

There was a postscript to this story. One day I got a call from a tabloid. The journalist asked me if I would give him a quote about a photograph of the Queen Mother playing pool. He said it was too late to send me the photograph (this was the days before the internet) but assured me that, judging by the image, she looked to be a very good player. I asked him how on earth I could give a comment on a photograph I had never seen. 'Believe me,' he said, 'I've seen the photograph and she looks like she can play.'

So I told him he could quote me as saying: 'She looks like she could have been a good player.' The next day I saw the newspaper, with the story right there on the front page. The photograph was her just holding a cue the way anyone else would. So my quote looked a bit daft in the context.

There was always another funny time just round the corner. I remember playing an exhibition once with Fred Davis. Everybody was trying to jazz the game up and I had the idea of wearing a white suit. The only trouble was, I didn't have white shoes, only black ones. So I got some of that white paint, the sort you would use on trainers, and used that to make them white. I turned up to the match dressed all in white, like something from *Randall and Hopkirk (Deceased)*. I always remember that when I came in to the venue Fred gave me a quizzical look. That look was matched the next morning when I went out for a run and returned wearing a bright-pink tracksuit. He must have wondered what on earth was going on.

I think that was the last time I ever ran, by the way.

The game needs a new Alex Higgins, for sure. When he walked from his seat to the table that was his stage. He could lose a frame but do so in such style that when he returned to his seat the applause would be such that you would have thought he had won it. He had a great presence at the table. His initial legacy was Jimmy White, although I was never sure how comfortable Jimmy was with the comparison. To be like Alex isn't easy. Ronnie O'Sullivan has that presence that Alex had as well. I wonder whether the next Alex Higgins might come from China. If you had asked me four years ago for a tip on who will win the World Championship in four years' time, my tip would have been Ding Junhui for sure. He has had such a meteoric rise in the game. I have also spoken with his manager. The expectation in China is unbelievable. There are 30 million people there watching him every time he plays. They put a lot of pressure on him. One time, when O'Sullivan beat him at Wembley, Ding left the venue in tears. He is a very, very good player but I would like to see him being a bit more extrovert when he comes to the table. That would help him. Then there is Liang Wenbo. He is a lot more attacking than Ding.

Ronnie O'Sullivan, to me, will be the catalyst for the new

Alex Higgins. Alex spawned Jimmy and Jimmy spawned Ronnie. Hopefully, Ronnie will spawn a new player who entertains and attacks. He makes it look so easy and it's all very fluent. That's why I would pay money to go and watch him play. I think he's an absolute genius. The only thing that can, in my opinion, sometimes let him down is that you sometimes get the feeling his heart is not in it. You would never say that about Alex, though. Nor Jimmy. I am not saying for one moment that Liang Wenbo has the skill and ability of O'Sullivan. I do see some panache in him though. That is what Alex did to make the game exciting and that is what Liang might yet bring to the game.

I see a lot of the English players coming through and some of them are very good. The problem is that a lot of them are so focused professionally that they are looking only for a way to win. That is not unreasonable, of course, but it does stifle them. Any sport needs a character who moves beyond that, someone with a little bit of 'X factor'. I had always seen Chinese players as very regimented, doing it by the book. Liang, however, takes it a bit further and hopefully he will help make the game exciting again. We wouldn't want everyone going that way. We need contrasts such as those we had between Alex and the likes of Griffiths and Reardon.

For the moment, O'Sullivan is our pearl. I hope that given the tremendous popularity of the game in China that somebody over there will spot how O'Sullivan plays and take the game to a new level of entertainment again. Without that, the game will continue to be hard work to watch. I'm not knocking those who play carefully. They have a living to earn and they want to succeed. For the good of the game, though, we need someone to step beyond that. Otherwise, television interest will dry up and then everyone will be in trouble. People keep telling me that Judd Trump, who comes from Bristol, is amazing. He still hasn't made the breakthrough, though. O'Sullivan and Hendry made their breakthroughs as teenagers. Clive Everton keeps telling me that Trump is the 'real deal', but he needs to get on with it. Taking everything into consideration, I think that the next Alex will come from China.

You may think, But what about all the bad things that came with the *last* Alex Higgins – the bad publicity, the controversy and so on? But when people talk about 'setting a good example for children' I always remember George Best and some of the things he did. I don't remember anyone saying then that he was a bad example to kids. If something is wrong, I think everyone knows it. I think any sport can cope with only one Alex Higgins, though. You wouldn't want more than that, you really wouldn't. He head-butted a tournament director, punched another in the stomach, was always slagging off the game. One Alex Higgins was enough, but less than one was not enough – because of the entertainment and attention he brought to the game.

To put it into context, we should consider where snooker

stands today. When Alex came along he made the game exciting, but Ted Lowe always used to say that he didn't think Alex was good for the game. I think he didn't want the way the game was played to be changed and he did want to protect snooker traditions. He thought the game was to be played by gentlemen in a gentlemanly manner. Alex was the first person to put a little wedge in that. Ted was also concerned about the amount of money that was beginning to come into the game. Now, I think we can all look at other sports and feel that a big injection of money spoilt them to a degree. Look at cricket and how speed has become of the essence. Everyone wants the game over quickly with a winning side. Alex's success was bringing money into the game and so who really was about to put their hand up and say, 'Stop – this is enough'? In snooker I think when we lost a big attraction when Alex retired. Fortunately, along came Jimmy White, who added some excitement.

OK, he has never won the World Championship (having lost each of the six finals he contested), but he carried the game during the 1990s. Stephen Hendry may have been winning all the titles, but I think that, without Jimmy battling away in his swashbuckling style, the game would not have had the same draw at all. Now we have Ronnie O'Sullivan as the jewel in the crown of the game. Ronnie is as talented a player as I have ever seen in my life but I don't think he has the same connection with the public as Alex and Jimmy had at their peaks.

If I were to compare Alex with a sportsman from another game it would probably be Seve Ballesteros, the star of golf. I always remember a clip of Colin Montgomerie when he was about to take a shot. Ballesteros walked up and told him what to do. Alex would have done that, he really would. Also, Ballesteros was very cavalier – hitting balls into car parks and the like. His body language was similar to Alex's, as well, as was his unpredictability.

Muhammad Ali is another sportsman comparable to Alex. He had that aura around him that convinced people that they were the greatest. Alex was never lacking in confidence, I remember him once signing an autograph 'Alexander the Great'. As we've seen, I don't go along with the George Best comparison. I never saw any major similarities. For a start, football is a team game. Alex was a bad loser and if he lost he would insult people, hit people – even head-butt people. It was his stage and if someone had knocked him off it he didn't like it.

Here is a story that illustrates this issue he had. We were doing an exhibition for Roger Lee in Ipswich. Alex knew a guy in Ipswich who ran a snooker club. Alex told me that his friend wanted us to go and play a few frames there in the afternoon. In return for our time, Alex said, his friend was going to give him an expensive television cabinet. It was a reproduction unit that would cost £1,000 at Harrods.

'That's nice,' I said.

'Don't worry, he'll give you £50 or something,' replied

Alex. On the way there we had a few drinks. The thing is, with Alex, when you start drinking you really start drinking. So we had a few drinks. The fella liked me and he said he would also give me one of the expensive television cabinets. Alex likes to feel special, so he was not amused by this moment of parity. 'No, give him £50,' he said. 'He'll be happy with £50.'

We were in this club all afternoon drinking away. We were fairly drunk by the time it came to go and do the exhibition. We were more or less poured into the car that took us there. We didn't even get changed. By the time we arrived the place was just packed. I was quite drunk when we got there. I was really struggling. Alex had gone off to the dressing room and when I got there to get him through for the show, I found him asleep on the sofa. I woke him up and said we had to get going. 'Oh, just go and play a few of the punters,' he said. 'I'll have a little sleep and join you in an hour.' I explained to him that it was him everyone had come to see, not me. 'Well, tell them to give me another 15 minutes,' he said and went straight back to sleep.

So I went through and said Alex wasn't feeling very well. 'He needs a bit of a rest then he'll be through,' I said. I think most people guessed what was really going on. Well, they would have done, seeing the state I was also in. So I played a few of the audience and for some reason – perhaps the drink I had inside me – the pockets seemed huge. They were like buckets – everything was going in for me! After a couple of frames I started to sense the audience getting agitated so I went back to the dressing room to try to rouse Alex.

I told him he had to get up and perform. He resisted for a while but eventually, with a sigh, said, 'Okay, where's my cue?' He got up with his hair all over the place and his clothes were all creased. He went out to play and he couldn't pot a ball. The problem is, with other people, if they cannot pot a ball they will find another way round it. They will have a joke or a chat with the audience. Not Alex, he was just sulking and glaring.

In a funny way, I think the audiences actually liked it. They wondered what was going to happen next. Someone would move in the audience and he would look up and snap: 'Keep still!' The unpredictability was exciting. During the interval that night I had a damp cloth and I was slapping him on the face with it to try to wake him up. I don't know where he got it from but in that second session he played great.

That was a typical day and night out with Alex. You just never knew what was going to happen next. He hated me in that first session when I was potting but he wasn't. He was an absolute nightmare, but then in the second half he was on fire and bags of fun. So it was unpredictability all along. You just never knew what was coming next. With most people in life, you almost invariably do know what you will get from them. With Alex, the opposite was the case. He would take you out of your routine or comfort zone with the click of a finger. It's like when that fella said he was going to give me a television cabinet. I knew in that instant that Alex was furious. From being the life and soul of the party a moment earlier, he now didn't want me to even be there. A bit later he shouted into my ear, 'I could have done the whole thing alone, you know? Then you'd have got fuck all!' What a charmer!

So part of the unpredictability was a bit nightmarish, but that was the price you paid for the excitement. At the end of that night we went back to the hotel. What does every single hotel in the world have? A night porter. What was Alex bound to do when he saw a night porter? Cause havoc. He could be a bloody nightmare to them. I could not help but feel sorry for them. He once smeared the handle of a vacuum cleaner with superglue. He thought that was really funny. Luckily, the man quickly let go of the handle when he realised something was amiss. Otherwise he could have had a real problem on his hands – quite literally.

Alex also loved having the night porters running around after him. He could be funny and charming with them, but only for as long as it took to convince them to do what he wanted them to do. They almost always knew who he was. In fact I was often amazed by the adulation he received from people across all parts of society. So he would charm them up to get them to rustle him up some food, even though the kitchen was closed. 'Come on,' he'd say, 'how about a quick sandwich?' He would charm them and charm them but the moment he got what he wanted out of them he would have a go at them. 'Go on, fuck off,' he'd say. He could charm the apple off a tree that man, but the moment he got the apple he could turn moody. You just never knew what to expect from him.

There was a time when he was playing at a club. He refused to sign autographs, even though there were lots of young kids queuing up for them. There was a little kid in a wheelchair and he tapped Alex on the shoulder, passed him a pound note and a pen and asked him to sign it for him. Alex put the pound note in his pocket, threw the pen away and walked off. The thing is when people tell this story they tend to be laughing, even though it was an unpleasant thing to do. People get so surprised by how outrageous he could be that they would laugh at his antics when they looked back on them. They would find them funny, even though things like this were clearly not funny at all. Alex wasn't trying to be funny when he did that, he was trying to be obnoxious and cruel.

Dennis Taylor always tells a funny story about another Higgins moment. Taylor was always very good at doing meet-and-greets with the game's sponsors. He knew what side his bread was buttered on and he knew how to conduct himself with the money-men. One day he played an exhibition match with Alex. Dennis had played some trick shots and Alex had looked as if he felt a bit left-out by the attention this brought Dennis' way. Afterwards, Dennis was busy chatting away with a sponsor and he could see over the sponsor's shoulder in the background that Alex was at the table. He was showing a few of the guests a few trick shots. Dennis kept half looking over the sponsor's shoulder at what Alex was getting up to at the table. All of a sudden, Alex was clearing up the table for the guys finished up with the white ball in the middle of the table between the blue and pink spots. Meanwhile, the black was on its spot. So he climbed up on to the table, with his legs in the air and said, 'I will double the black in the top pocket.' He whacked the black ball as hard as he possibly could. Then, he tried to roll across the table to get out of the way of the ball. The trouble is that he got his foot stuck in the pocket and the ball bounced back and whacked him in the crotch.

Meanwhile, poor Dennis was trying to have an intelligent conversation with the sponsor and all the while he could see Alex doubled-up on the table, clutching himself. That's the sort of mayhem that Alex was capable of creating. Who else would try to roll across the table like that? Years later I tried to re-enact it for a video I was making. I didn't manage to pull off the roll successfully but at least I didn't get my foot stuck in the pocket. He was a one-off, was Alex.

CHAPTER 11

THIS WAS
MY LIFE

I had a lot to be grateful to Alex for. Without him there wouldn't have been anyone for me to start with on my impressions. Then came Griffiths, Taylor and others. That's how I got the gig on *Big Break*, because of my impersonations. They got me on because of my sense of humour. I used to put the Willie Thorne bald wig on, or the Dennis Taylor glasses. In the early shows that was what we did. Through being on *Big Break* I met Jim Davidson and got a wider light-entertainment career. This included getting gigs in pantomime. It all came from him. He gave me that vision that you could spread your wings.

As a result of my fame, I got an appearance on the legendary television show *This Is Your Life*. I never realised that was so PR-led. I had no idea that publicity agents could get you on there to promote a video. That was basically how I got on there. I was releasing a snooker video and they had a word with ITV suggesting me as a subject. I remember that I had done a few appearances as a guest on *This Is Your Life*. For instance, I was the person who 'caught' Jimmy when he was the subject. As far as I was concerned, Jimmy thought he and I were about to play an exhibition in Richmond. So I went along to meet him, knowing that the show's host, Michael Aspel, would appear with the famous red book. It was all set to be a big surprise.

What I found out only afterwards was that Alex had rung Jimmy the evening before and told him what had been set up. It's amazing the secrecy they surround the whole thing with. They swear everyone to secrecy. Alex, though, couldn't resist blabbing it to Jimmy, whom he called 'Wind' (a derivative of his nickname Whirlwind). So he had phoned him and said, 'Oh, just to let you know, Wind, you're on *This Is Your Life* tomorrow. I'm only telling you because I don't want you to be too shocked.' Unbelievable. It reminds me of when Alex was the subject of the show.

Del Simmons was the contracts negotiator in snooker and a larger-than-life character. They had booked all us guests into a hotel near the studio. I went up to reception and said, 'The name's Virgo and there's a room booked for me.'

The fellow behind the counter spoke very little English, which seems to be the case more and more in London hotels, don't you find? He said, 'No — no Virgo here.'

So I called Del over and told him what the problem was. He was a good guy to have on your side at times like this. He told the hotel guy, 'I've spoken to the host of *This Is Your Life* and he said you were going to give Mr Virgo the best suite in the hotel.'

The guy got a bit flustered and said, 'The only suite booking I've got here is a Mr Watkins.'

Simmons turned to me with a straight face and said, 'Watkins? Isn't he drilling for you in Saudi Arabia?' Anyway, I ended up with the best suite in the hotel!

When Alex did the show it was a strange night. Suzi Quatro was one of the guests and he kept asking her for £400, which he said she owed him after a game of snooker they had played. Also, he wasn't getting on very well with his wife Lynn at the time. Indeed, they were having a fight back at the hotel. We went over to see what was going on and he told us to leave them alone.

When it was my turn for *This Is Your Life* I was taken by surprise. I suppose you could say I've been a little gullible about such things. Noel Edmonds successfully did me twice with a 'Gotcha Oscar'. The first time, I had fallen hook, line and sinker for the ruse that the band Right Said Fred wanted to record a single with me. It was to be a new version of their famous single 'I'm Too Sexy'. My manager had convinced me it was serious and was going to be a big Christmas hit. I was singing lines like 'I'm too sexy with my beard on, I'm too sexy for Ray Reardon.' Naturally, it was all a wind-up, but I didn't mind. When you're in the fame game it's all good publicity and helpful for your profile.

So I got a phone call that there was to be a contestant on *The Generation Game* who was a big fan of mine and wanted to meet me. I drove to the studios and walked onto the set as asked. Jim Davidson, my former co-host on *Big Break*, was the host. He was talking to the contestant about how much she liked me when all of a sudden I burst through a sheet of paper and onto the set. She was screaming and I gave her a cuddle. The next thing I know Michael Aspel is walking on set with his famous red book. I never thought it was anything to do with me. For a start, I was always of the belief that once you had been divorced twice it would not work practically to build a show around you. How on earth could they? I thought. But, sure enough, he walked up and said, 'John Virgo, this is your life!' It was such a shock.

They drove me to the studios in Teddington and I actually felt not unlike the Bob Hoskins character at the end of the gangster film *The Long Good Friday*. The IRA have got him in the back of the car and they are taking him away against his will. I felt much the same. All these thoughts were going through my head about who might turn up in the show, who would be sitting next to me in the studio. I was living with a woman at the time and I was thinking, Will the ex-wife object to my daughter being there? and a million other thoughts. Once I got to the studios they handed me a glass of champagne and I felt a bit better. Finally, the time came for us to do the show. There were two spare seats next to where I was going to sit. I knew that was going to be for my daughter and my son. Then my siblings and other relatives and friends came in one by one.

Next up some of my friends and colleagues from the game of snooker joined us. Alex was, naturally, one of them. When he walked on we had a big hug and he shook my hand. As he was doing so he whispered into my year: 'You're still a cunt.' Nobody else could hear him say it, thank God. But that is what he said. Outrageous. I was talking to Michael Aspel later and it turned out that my show had the highest viewing figures for the entire series. This was partly because the moment when Aspel first walked up to me had been shown live on *The Generation Game*. I was still very proud of that rating, though. It was amazing, really. I still found it all a bit contrived in terms of the publicity aspect of it. I had grown up watching war heroes on the show, men who had saved people's lives. Yet here I was basically plugging a video. The bit I will always remember was Alex calling me a 'cunt'. Typical of him.

CHAPTER 12

FINAL DAYS

As I've said, none of us expected Alex to live to a ripe old age. He just had that aura around him that hinted at an untimely end. All the same, we were all devastated when we learned he had cancer.

I first learned of Alex's illness the same way as most other people: I read it in a newspaper. The poor man's world had fallen apart when he was diagnosed with cancer of the throat, palate and neck nodes. He went through a seven-week course of radiotherapy, which he described as 'truly horrible'. As he battled back from that first bout of illness he was living alone, by his own decision. Everyone did their best to keep his spirits up. We thought Alex had made a full recovery and we thought, Great! But then we did some shows and he was so painfully thin. I remember, going back a while, if you saw anybody who had lost weight, you'd think, Bloody hell, they're ill. You didn't assume they were deliberately on a diet to lose weight.

When I saw Alex I said to Jimmy, 'I thought you said he'd been given the all-clear.'

Jimmy said, 'Yes, he has been given the all-clear.' But I think what had happened was that he had given up on life and that was that.

You know how you used to hear that phrase about somebody dying 'of old age'. You never hear that any more, do you? Nowadays people give some sort of specific medical reason. But I think what old age means is that you've lived your life and you realise there is not a future for you. I think with Alex he had just had enough and had given up. What had made him get up and out of bed in the morning – snooker and fame – wasn't there any more. He didn't even have much money left for his other passion – horseracing and gambling.

Yes, he could go and play an exhibition but, as we saw at his last one, he hardly had any energy. This was a man who had once been able to send the ball flying round the table. He could do things with a snooker ball I had never dreamed of. Now he could hardly pick up the cue, and when he did he couldn't screw the ball back more than a quarter of an inch. He looked shocking – like a skeleton. This all left a bitter taste in my mouth. What was he? A freak show? I didn't like seeing somebody I so admired this way.

So I think in the end he just lost his dignity, and that would have been a big problem for Alex. I think maybe he decided he had had enough of everything. He had pushed at so many boundaries, but, if he had not done so, then we might not be talking about him as a man who broke barriers and changed the game. People did charity nights for him at the end and raised money for him, which showed how much affection there still was for the man. It was touching, in a way, yet I know that some of these people, had they seen him walk into a room, would walk out of the other door to avoid him. I hope that most people in the game were grateful to him for what he did to snooker.

There was a stage show put on about the life of Alex, called *Hurricane*. It even went to America. On the opening night I went along with Jimmy White and Rolling Stones guitarist Ronnie Wood. When we arrived Alex was there and he came and sat with us. As the play went along he was always one step ahead, telling us what was going to happen next because he had seen the rehearsals already. The main theme was how drink and other things had ruined his life. But there was one final line, which they could only have got from Alex himself. 'WPBSA,' the Alex character cried, 'why did you ruin my life?' And then the lights went out dramatically. I thought, What a load of bollocks.

This is the crux of the question of what went wrong for Alex. Did the authorities ruin his life, or did he ruin it himself? Maybe you could say we *did* ruin his life. We could have banned him earlier, for instance. We could have given him not so much as a slap on the wrists as a firm pointer, telling him, 'You cannot behave like this. We appreciate your talent and what you have brought to the game, but you have to change.'

Instead, we pussyfooted around with him. I think the truth was that the sport needed him badly. They say nobody is bigger than any game, but the fact is that we did need him. He was once asked if he could live without the game of snooker. His answer? 'Could snooker live without me?' This was typical Alex arrogance but it was not without truth. He breathed life into the game. I was getting bored of snooker before he came along and there seemed no future in the game. Had I said to my boss in that office, who told me I would end up selling shoelaces in the park, that I was going to become a professional snooker player he would have laughed at me.

There was no way Stephen Hendry, for instance, would have earned £8 million in prize money without Alex making the game watchable and making it a really exciting prospect for television and sponsors. Even when he did not reach the latter stages of the competitions it was Alex who had been the initial draw.

So, did the snooker governing bodies let him down? It's a question I often consider. Maybe we could have jumped on his worst excesses faster and helped him stay more on the straight and narrow. But without all that wildness the game would not have generated the headlines and the publicity it so badly needed. The game needed that attention to succeed. It was no use snooker being stuck tucked away in the third page from the back of the newspapers. We needed front-page attention to draw in the interest and therefore the finance. That was the dilemma. The authorities didn't want him to create more problems, but at the same time they didn't want to ban him for fear that those seeds he had sown in the game, which were beginning to bring forth shoots, might wither away. These shoots were the first sign that the game was becoming properly known. We could have just dampened down that fever if we hadn't been careful. Without Alex we would have been struggling for a figurehead. Certainly, Davis or Griffiths could not have carried the game in quite the same way.

When I saw Alex play I found a new side to the game that was exhilarating. Here at last was a real character in a game that had, in truth, been very short of them. Sometimes, though, there is no accounting for taste. I once had a conversation with a man who had stopped watching snooker. I asked him why. 'There are no characters in the game any more,' he told me. So I asked him who his favourite character of the past had been, expecting him to say Alex Higgins or Jimmy White.

'That's easy,' he said. 'Terry Griffiths.' I didn't know what to say to that!

It is hard to know what other people want sometimes,

but I knew what I wanted – and that was Alex Higgins. Alex's impact had been immediate, though. I remember shortly after he appeared on the circuit that I visited a snooker club in South Wales. Previously such clubs had been tranquil, polite and not heavily populated places. But now they were suddenly packed out with people racing round the table, bumping into one another. This was the impact of Alex writ large. The game was no longer ruled by gentlemanly considerations. Instead it was about passion and wowing the audience. Great stuff.

Alex could be a bad loser and he never accepted second billing under any circumstances. Once I found fame with *Big Break*, snooker fans would sometimes come to me first for an autograph. But when I was out with Jim Davidson, they would go to him first. There was a pecking order. That could upset some people, and Alex was one of those people. In fact, if he wasn't asked first he was more than likely to tell them to piss off. He needed to be the centre of attention. For me the best saying in sport is that the only thing worse than a bad loser is a bad winner. I can understand bad losers, but I don't understand bad winners. But in sport now the overexuberant celebration just seems to be part and parcel of winning. There once was a day when, if you scored a goal in football, you shook hands and that was it. Now, though, they run to the crowd, rip their shirts off and go berserk. It's rubbing salt in the wound of your opponent, isn't it? I know Jimmy White always found it hard to see his opponent celebrating too much. It's like a personal insult. You've won the game, why do you need to rub it in? But that just seems to be an accepted thing in sport now.

Alex was certainly a bad loser – a terrible one actually. Was he a bad winner? No, I don't think he was. As I've said before, he thought that everyone had come to see him. As far as he was concerned everyone else involved with the game, including his opponent on the day, was just part of a supporting cast. They were just a filler for him. Everybody was there only to see him, he thought. In most cases he was right. He gave them what they wanted: excitement. That's why it took him ten years to win his second World Championship, because he was inconsistent and busy entertaining.

Is it better to have Alex, an entertainer, or to have a Steve Davis, or a Stephen Hendry, who wins everything? The pages of the record books may remember Davis and Hendry, but in people's hearts it will always be Alex. Success does not necessarily endear you to the public, particularly in Britain. The mentality here is sometimes suspicious of success. Look at how people are about Manchester United's success. Lots of people hate them for it.

Alex was a bad loser, though. He had an army of excuses to draw on if he lost. It was everybody's fault apart from his own. He would complain to the referee that he had heard him breathing and been put off. Or it would be because somebody had moved in his line of sight. That was rich coming from him. Once, while his opponent was busy at the table, Alex started polishing his shoes with the cloths that are left out for players to wipe their cues with. So he didn't mind creating a bit of drama on the side himself.

In 1990, Alex made his last appearance at the Crucible. In his first-round match he was beaten by Steve James 10–5. In the mid-session interval of that match, instead of going back to his dressing room, Alex sat in his chair. Looking at him, I couldn't help but feel sorry for him. His game wasn't up to standard and, worse, he had come to the championship surrounded by controversy. He had recently threatened to have Dennis Taylor 'shot the next time you are in Northern Ireland' after a row developed between them at another tournament. The Irish team had got to the final, where they would play Canada. Before the match, Higgins called a meeting with Taylor and the other member of the team, Tommy Murphy. They met in the ladies' toilet, because Alex was worried that they might be overheard in the men's.

During the meeting, Alex explained his strategy. They would each play two frames and the last two of the afternoon would be played by Dennis. This meant that Alex would play more frames in the evening. To Dennis, this was typical glory-hunting behaviour from Alex. However, he went along with it for a quiet life. In his two frames against

Alain Robidoux, Alex won the first but lost the second. He decided then that he, and not Dennis, would now play the last two frames of the afternoon – despite the fact that Dennis was dressed, cue in hand, ready to play. He lost both frames and Northern Ireland after the first session were already 6–2 behind. At the end of the afternoon session Taylor's 71 break was still the front-runner for the £6,000 highest-break prize. If it stood, Taylor told us, he had no intentions of sharing it – Higgins had the highest break the year before and said he wouldn't share it. Normally in team snooker any money won is shared by all the players equally. It didn't really matter what Taylor had planned, because in the last frame of the match Robidoux made a fantastic 124 break to win the prize himself. Canada, meanwhile, beat Northern Ireland 9–5. Well, in the post-match press conference Alex went into overdrive.

'In my estimation, Dennis Taylor is not a snooker person,' he said. 'He is a money person. The more he gets the more he wants, he will never be sated. He puts money before country. He belongs back in Coalisland [in County Tyrone]. He's not fit to wear this badge – the red hand of Ulster.'

This was a typical petulant outburst from Alex. I was there at that tournament and felt very sorry for Dennis. It was apparent then that, coupled with his loss of form and the frustration that ensued, Alex was becoming a danger both to himself and to everyone else. Well, when Taylor heard about what Alex had said he decided to stage a press conference of his own. His voice shaking with emotion, he talked about how hurt he was by Alex's outburst but also revealed something sensational that Alex had said to him backstage, 'I come from the Shankill,' Alex had told Taylor, 'you come from Coalisland. The next time you're in Northern Ireland I'll have you shot.' Taylor was visibly shaken – well you would be, wouldn't you?

'I've known Alex since 1968, when he came over to Blackburn. I found a flat for him to stay in. I got a television put in for him. I did my best to help him.' He continued, 'I was literally shaking when I went out to play tonight. Two days after I won the world title I had the best reception I've ever had in my life in the Shankill Leisure Centre. I have never got involved in the politics.'

John Spencer, the new chairman of the Association, confirmed, 'There was a load of abuse fired at Dennis.'

I suppose that something was bound to happen in that tournament. You could just feel the tension in the air. After the semi-final Alex had said, 'If I'm not captain tomorrow, I'm not playing.' The kind of threat that we in the game had got used to over the years, it was, as usual, a lot of hot air. The reason he wasn't captain was that the highest-ranked player had that honour and that player was Dennis Taylor. That was the thing with Alex: even though he was at this point on the decline, he still really believed that *everybody* was behind him. So the 1990 championship was his swansong, but, as in everything, he didn't go quietly.

It had been his last appearance at the Crucible and everything was closing in on him. On his way to the press conference he punched the press officer in the stomach. He then sat down and proceeded to announce his retirement from the game and referred to snooker as 'the most corrupt game in the world' and also alluded to some 'incest' going on behind the scenes.

In all honesty, the game was getting very incestuous backstage. It seemed that people were having affairs left, right and centre. It was an incestuous kind of atmosphere, anyway. We were all in Sheffield for the best part of three weeks, staying in the same hotel and drinking at the same bar late into the night. The press conference was fed through to monitors backstage. He was doing an interview and we were all sitting backstage. Around us were lots of people whom Alex was alluding to. He could be a good drinker, but he could sometimes overstate the fact that he had a good drink. All of a sudden in the press conference he suddenly started referring to these 'incestuous' goings on. I sensed that a lot of people around me were becoming very uncomfortable. I'm sure a few of them wished we could turn the sound down. I think even in the wake of it people were concerned that once he had left the sport he might write a real 'warts-and-all' book, exposing all the details of the game. People really were nervous about this.

Jimmy White was once asked if he had any skeletons in the cupboard. 'Skeletons?' he answered. 'I've got a graveyard.' We were ordinary working-class people who went out for a drink and enjoyed having a good time. None of us were whiter than white. We did what people did. Then, all of a sudden a few years into the Crucible era, there were not only sports reporters at the tournaments but also feature writers and news reporters. They were sniffing round for a bit of scandal. I believe this was to the detriment of the game. There were rumours that people would be selling stories on other people in the game, just to save their own skin. This created a lot of suspicion and paranoia for most players. Alex was not so bothered, because he didn't care about anything, as he showed in that press conference. For the rest of us it was more of a worry. We were definitely minding our Ps and Qs. It almost got to the stage when we became frightened to go out. The atmosphere at the hotel we stayed at used to be great, but now it was more sombre.

The content itself during that infamous press conference was often very rambling, but every so often he would refer to an affair that might be going on and I could feel people getting nervous. However, even when he was rambling, Alex had a genius about him. At one point he said, 'The game is tripe and that is nothing against Northern people, who like tripe – I enjoy tripe myself.' We were seeing the ramblings of a strange kind of genius. There should have been a cooling-off period after the matches finished. The opposite was true: the players would be ushered through to the press. That, in effect, was just fanning the flames for a character like Alex.

Whether anybody by this time was taking what Alex said seriously I do not know, but it all certainly made for good headlines, as you can imagine. SNOOKERED BY BIRDS, BOOZE AND BRAWLING was the *Daily Star*'s offering. Most newspapers went to town on the story and many strung together a list of Alex's misdemeanours. Some read almost like obituaries. A journalist in the now defunct *Today* newspaper remarked, 'Hurricanes always blow themselves out in the end, even self-invented, self-inflated versions like Alex Higgins.' The *Daily Star* even said that a movie was going to be made of his life: 'Top actor John Hurt is tipped to star as the fiery snooker star Alex "Hurricane" Higgins on-screen. Oscar-nominated Hurt is said to be "desperate to play the part".'

It was a sad day for Alex, but in many ways it was sad for the game of snooker, too. Unfortunately, given Alex's well-fingered self-destruct button, it could not have ended any other way. The same year saw the retirement of the great Fred Davis OBE. It seemed that the early 1990s would see many top names fade away from the game as the future of snooker was grasped by new hands. Stephen Hendry was obviously the man for the 1990s. Steve Davis was still a force. It was Jimmy 'Whirlwind' White, though, who would take over the Higgins mantle in the wake of his retirement; after the Hurricane, the Whirlwind.

Although the 1990s will be remembered by most for the seven world titles claimed by Stephen Hendry, for me it was Jimmy White who kept the game popular. True, he has never won a World Championship but what a contribution he has made to the game of snooker! He has won everything possible in the game apart from that coveted title in Sheffield. Why is this? In my mind there are a number of reasons. In his semi-final against Alex in 1982 he was leading 15–14. But then Alex produced the best break I have ever seen. Had Jimmy won that match I feel sure he would have also won in the final against Reardon. That's not to take anything away from Reardon, who had won the world title six times, but I felt he was on the way down at that point. Then, in his first final, where he could have become the youngest-ever winner, he lost to Steve Davis. He had been 12–4 down after the first two sessions and made a tremendous comeback to lose by only 18–16. Little could he know then that it would be another seven years before he would reach the final of the tournament again.

Alex had always been a big influence on White. This is understandable because White loved the way he played. I also think that White liked the way that Alex dealt with authority figures in the game. It is the same as with the likes of George Best and tennis ace John McEnroe – something about these sorts of figures excites something inside young people. I always felt, though, that in taking over the Higgins mantle White occasionally got carried away with the whole

Higgins thing. I suppose his problem was that, although he was a great natural talent like Alex, as personalities they were actually worlds apart. Socially, Alex was always in control, whereas Jimmy was more easily led. Mixing late nights with playing top-class snooker – particularly over the 17 days of a World Championship – is a recipe for disaster.

So the seven years that it took White to reach a final again were wasted. There was just no reason – on ability – that he should not have won the World Championship at least three or four times. I remember 1988, when he lost to Terry Griffiths. I spoke to him halfway through that match, about the way he was breaking the balls open from the break. Normally you hit the last or second-last red of the pyramid. That way you get a good safety and bring out a few reds. For some reason best known to himself he was breaking off by hitting the second red below the pink. This was something you would normally do only if you were practising or perhaps if you were playing an exhibition match. To do this in a World Championship, particularly against as seasoned and experienced a campaigner as Griffiths, was little short of suicidal. It proved that way in the match: Jimmy lost and Griffiths marched on to the final. After all his years in the game Jimmy still had not learned.

So I think his main problem was that he relied too much on his talent at potting – but there is so much more to snooker than potting balls. His next final came in 1991, when he met John Parrott. Surely this was to be his chance.

He lost the first session 7–0, but he couldn't actually be blamed at all. Parrott simply produced seven of the best frames ever played at the Crucible. Again, Jimmy was not to win the final, but it seemed that the penny had finally dropped and he started to couple his great potting with good safety play. The trouble was that he had, in horseracing terms, a lot of miles on the clock.

Stephen Hendry was improving all the time and would prove too strong. Twice in his final against Hendry, Jimmy looked the likely winner. Leading 14–10 going into the final session he looked certain to win, only to lose 18–14. Shortly after that final I was at lunch with Hendry and we were talking about the match. He commented that Jimmy's cue-ball control wasn't very good. 'Neither was yours at 14–8 down,' I replied. Unfortunately, Jimmy couldn't go in for the kill and instead watched as Hendry created history by winning 10 frames in a row.

In the wake of Alex's retirement my results, apart from some odd exceptions, were not getting any better. In 1990 I had signed with a new management team. It consisted of two ex-1960s pop stars. Although my snooker was not good, and after what had happened politically I was not comfortable at the tournaments, I actually had a more immediate problem facing me. As I've explained earlier, if you are not winning in snooker then you do not earn money. True, there is always exhibition work, but certainly not as much as you would get from winning tournaments.

Also, if you were not doing well then you would not be getting as much screen time on television and would as a consequence be invited to exhibitions less and less.

In 1991 I made my final appearance at the Crucible. I was playing Tony Knowles and during the first mid-session interval I led 4–0. I was playing really well. You can imagine my surprise, then, when one of my new management team, Troy Dante, came into my dressing room and said, 'Keep going, you're boring him to death.' As a fan of Alex Higgins, I had always prided myself on being an attacking player. So Troy's statement was the last thing I wanted to hear. Sadly, I lost the match and I didn't realise then that this was the last time I would walk through those famous curtains of the Crucible.

So many snookering legends and eras have come to an end of late. Tragically, so did Alex's life. Even when he beat the initial burst of throat cancer it was not a full triumph for him, because the life that he loved and craved was no longer there for him. That adulation and fame that the game gave him, not to mention the adrenalin rush of being in the front line and under the spotlight, had all disappeared. When he came out to take part in the Legends tour in Sheffield you could see a mile off how weak he was. Jimmy spoke for us all when he said how frustrating it was to see this great battler give up. Alex had always been as brave as a lion and he had just lost that.

The last time I saw him play was at that Legends tour. Then, a few weeks later at a charity night in Manchester, I saw him again. He was having fun, dancing on the stage and enjoying the limelight he craved. People should not criticise those who love the limelight. Alex gave as good as he took. He contributed so much to the game and entertained people in spades. Anyway, he was in his element that evening as the centre of attention. The big screen had shown his famous 69 break. It was a nice sight to see him enjoying that limelight; he was at his very impish best. Later in the evening a photograph was taken of Alex, Jimmy, Tony Knowles and me together on the stage. I was not to know it at the time, of course, but that was the last occasion I saw Alex alive. He would soon – seemingly – give up on life.

He was living alone in a small flat in Ireland and I suppose that, zestful as he was that night when he returned home, he must have lost all that magic. There was so little in his eyes for him to live for, I think. The things that made him come alive as a person had pretty much disappeared. So he just gave up, which as Jimmy said was so frustrating for those of us who knew and loved him best. It is as if he had filled his life up with so much excitement that what was left for him in the future just wasn't enough. He liked to live in the fast lane and do off-the-wall things. Take those away from him and he lost his lust for life. We've all been there, I think, at some stage in our lives. For my own part, after my divorce I felt very down and wondered what would happen next, even what *could* happen next. For Alex, his true love was snooker and entertaining the public. Now that love affair was no longer an option, and he realised that. Try as he might, he just couldn't perform any more. You might think, Why didn't he just go and enjoy a happy retirement? But what happy retirement was on the cards for Alex? He had no money left. I look at what some golfers earn today and some of them, after a few years of playing, have earned enough never to have to work again in their lives. That wasn't the case for Alex. He was skint.

Sometimes men try to lighten the tension when they are with a sick friend by employing a bit of 'gallows humour'. But Alex wasn't the type of person you would feel comfortable making a joke to if he was the subject of the joke. He simply wasn't that type of person. Alex certainly had a sense of humour, a wicked and sharp one at times. But it evaporated if the jokes were pointed at him. He could be very, very aggressive with people who tried that. I was shocked by his appearance and I did feel sympathy for him, but I basically didn't refer to how he looked. I just tried to let him get on with it. He wasn't looking for sympathy. Humour was another of the things that diminished in him by the end. Alex was a very intelligent and witty man, he could make some razor-sharp comments and observations. He was a genius of a person. He really could come out with some very cutting remarks. But by the end of his life it was impossible to understand what he was saying most of the time. He could hardly speak. That was another sad thing.

People began to rally round him again. Charity fundraisers were arranged. He had lost his teeth during his cancer treatment, so people raised money for him to get dental work done, as he had been living on baby food. Funnily enough I think the only things that kept him going for a while were the two pots: the kind you smoke and the kind that holds a pint of Guinness. It was hard for us to see him in the state he was in at the end. Still, I remember seeing him dancing round on the stage that night and I was thinking, Yeah, he's having a good time. So at least in that sense it was a nice final memory to have of him.

Then one day the phone call that I had dreaded finally came. Jimmy rang me and announced that Alex had passed away. The newspapers quickly started phoning, asking for my reaction. I told them all mostly the same thing. I said that it was so very sad that Alex had gone and that I wanted to say a big thank you to him for all he did. He gave us all an opportunity to make a good living from the game. Before he came along it was just a parlour game. No one could ever dream that you could become a millionaire playing snooker. But Alex gave us that belief; whether we achieved it or not was up to us. It's a short-term career, like many sports. So that belief he gave us was key. Some of the old school such as Ted Lowe were unhappy about the money that came into the game. But 'Corinthian spirit' only gets you so far.

After Alex had won the World Championship in 1982, interest rocketed again. The next thing we knew there were 18.5 million viewers watching the 1985 final between Davis and Taylor into the early hours of the morning. That was what Alex had done, so his death truly was a sad end to a great talent. This may be a strange analogy, but I always remember that there was a racehorse that looked as if it could have been tailor-made to run in the Grand National. But the trainer said, 'There is no way I would run a horse of mine in the National.' Yet had that horse run in the Grand National it would have won it and been remembered for ever and ever. In the end, that's all that's left, isn't it? What you do for people to remember you outside of your family is an achievement. Alex will be remembered by me as a genius and someone who brought snooker into the sporting world. He will always be remembered for being instrumental in that. Sad as the ending was, he will be remembered, and that always means that he did something with his life.

I just hope that when people look back on that life they remember the good times. Like that 69 break he made against Jimmy White. That should be his epitaph. It showed what he was capable of when he was at the top of his game. In the wake of his death, I thought back over my dealings with him. One of my earliest memories was when he came along to an amateur night I was at. I was playing Ray Reardon and Alex came as a guest to play some exhibition games. He was already building a major reputation and he was suddenly being invited to play exhibition games. I was already a major player on the amateur circuit so at first I wondered why this Higgins guy from Belfast was being invited to play exhibition games.

The moment he walked in and started playing I could see why – it was like watching Rudolf Nureyev dance. It really was. Even when he put his leg up on the table to reach a long shot he did it with grace. His mannerisms were so graceful. I got it, I really got it. When he walked up to the table to take his turn, it was as if the table were his stage. That's how much theatre he brought to the game. He had a flamboyant style. By the time he finished the crowd would give him a standing ovation. Not that he was the quickest player. The quickest was actually Tony Drago, the Maltese player. He was even faster than Alex. When he played in a club in Malta there was a marble floor. He walked round the table so quickly that it was like watching Fred Astaire tap-dance. But, as I say, for Alex the table was his stage. He never apologised for the flamboyance and theatre he brought to the game, and nor should he have done. When he was on form, he had the audience eating out of the palm of his hand. If he wasn't playing well he'd have an excuse, anyway. It's so sad that someone who brought so much pleasure, entertainment and joy to so many people should lose his life so early.

It came as a bit of a shock when I was told he had died because only three years before Jimmy had told me Alex had the all-clear. I was sad to hear of his death, of course, but in a way I got the feeling that at the end that may have been what he wanted. It was his life and he had always lived it the way he wanted to. Jimmy was keeping me up to date with the arrangements. To be honest, I was in two minds about whether I should even go to the funeral. First of all, it wasn't out of any disrespect but, as I heard more and more comments from people in the aftermath of Alex's passing, I sensed a lot of hypocrisy in the air. There was this sudden interest in him from a game that, though I wouldn't say it had turned his back on him, had not seemed really interested in him in the latter years of his life.

When they had the 25th anniversary of the sponsorship of Embassy, he wasn't invited as a past Champion. Jimmy had been encouraging Alex to get back practising so they could do a few exhibition matches together. However, as far as people from the game were concerned, he was pretty much a lone friend for Alex. Most of the rest of the game had forgotten him. Then suddenly, when Alex died, there were people coming out of the woodwork and saying great things about him.

So, when I thought about the funeral, I wondered whether I should go. I realised that there would be a lot of mayhem and frenzy around it. It was Jimmy who persuaded me. It was during one of our many telephone conversations at this time that I shared with him my doubts. 'How can you *not* go?' he asked. 'Given how you felt about him and all you went through, you really should go and pay your last respects to him.' I realised he was right, so I decided to go.

It was an early start for me that day. My wife Rosie had to drive me to the airport at 4 am. I then shared a taxi from the airport to Belfast city centre with the young snooker player Shaun Murphy. When I arrived I noticed there was some discussion afoot about who hadn't come. Maybe they had valid reasons for not being there, but, if not, you would have thought they would have made the effort. I decided to go straight to the cathedral rather than go to Alex's house. I arrived early in the area and there was already a bit of a crowd and buzz gathering, but at first nothing spectacular. So I went and sat in a coffee shop, waiting the start time.

Then, all of a sudden, we got word that the cortège had begun its procession, so we walked back round the corner to the cathedral. The streets were lined with crowds. Belfast had come out to pay its respects. It was very moving to see such a throng. On a less uplifting note there were also a lot of media people. There were numerous camera crews with reporters sticking their microphones up my nose, asking for soundbites. I wasn't there for that. I was there to pay my last respects to my hero Alex. 'How do you feel?' they would ask. What a question! However, there was a big emotional crowd gathering and as I looked at it, taking in the atmosphere, I suddenly wondered how on earth I could ever have considered *not* going to the funeral. Witnessing the reaction made me realise that going along was the only option.

I saw lots of familiar faces from the world of snooker that I hadn't seen for many years. Then the carriage arrived outside bearing Alex's coffin. As the coffin was removed from this carriage, which had been pulled by two black horses, it was almost like a scene from *The Magnificent Seven*. They brought the coffin out and people started applauding. That seems to be the new thing now, applause rather than silence.

Then above the applause rose cheers and cries of 'Come on, Alex!' It was just the sort of things that people shouted to him to encourage him when he played snooker.

'Good old Higgy!' others added. Even I started applauding, even though I'm not a natural for responding that way at a funeral. Then a wreath was brought through that had 'The People's Champion' spelt out in flowers. That increased the volume of the applause even more. It was a great send-off.

The Dean of Belfast, Houston McKelvey, read a tribute out on behalf of Jimmy White. 'Only a year ago, Alex was talking about playing again and coming on the road with me,' said the tribute. 'It angers me that he never listened to anyone, close friends or family but that was Alex. He was an individual, his own man, he was the Hurricane. I will miss him to the end.' So will I.

As I left the church a lot of people approached me. Some thanked me for coming, others were still asking whether he really played those shots in the famous video (details of which you can read about in the epilogue). It was just a sad day. Funerals are always sad. Even though there was applause and a bit of shouting it was still a sombre day. I got caught up in conversations outside and, by the time I had finished, there were no more cars going to the burial. So I decided to walk alone to the reception at the Europa Hotel. It was an emotional experience, that walk. All along the way people were shouting things out to me. 'Hello John, thanks for coming,' they would shout. 'What a great man he was, eh John?' Just amazing! The city loved him.

When I got to the reception there were a few people there who had also not gone to the burial. After a while we wondered what had happened to those who had, for they seemed to be taking a long time over it. When we found out what had happened we couldn't help but raise an eyebrow and think, Only Alex could have this happen at his funeral. It turns out there had been a mix-up over times at the cemetery. The upshot was that they had arrived half an hour earlier than the time the staff had been expecting to do the burial. So the mourners ended up standing there for 30 agonising minutes waiting for the staff to be ready to lay

Alex's body to rest. It was unusual for Alex to arrive half an hour early for anything, but he managed it in death. There's an irony there somewhere.

Once we all gathered at the reception we just did what people normally do at funerals. We spoke about our memories of him and we commiserated with his family. Then this tip went round about a horse, so we went to Alex's favourite bookmakers, which was across the road from the hotel, and placed bets on it. 'Come on, Alex,' we shouted at the horse. Sure enough, it won the race. I had this strange feeling that he was watching over us as we cheered. In my imagination he was pulling a wry smile and saying, 'Well, isn't that just my luck to get a winner when I can no longer put a bet on it!'

It had been a day of mixed emotions but it was certainly a good send-off for a great man. He had been open about the fact that he wanted his funeral to be a bigger and better send-off than the one George Best had got. That famous Belfast boy had been laid to rest in style in 2005, but by all accounts Alex got his wish, because his send-off was widely considered to have been a bigger occasion. I wasn't surprised by how grand the occasion was, because I knew what the people of Belfast thought of him. The Irish loved him; there are few people in the world more loving of a rebellious character than the Irish. It goes beyond them, though. He was loved by so many people from all parts of the world and all walks of life. I think the reason for this goes beyond snooker. I think there is a little rebel inside all of us. A voice that wants to say, 'Stop telling me what to do, let me do my own thing.' There is a part of us that thinks we are bigger than any rules or regulations. We all have moments when we have had enough of authority, when we don't want to conform any longer. For all Alex's faults, he did show us that you don't have to conform to everything all the time.

Even as a child, I can remember during school holidays we would sometimes climb over the school fence to play football in the school grounds. I loved it, but I was also always thinking that at any moment some figure of authority would discover us and that we would be in desperate trouble. Of course, there would never be really bad trouble on the cards. At worst we would get a bit of a ticking-off and be sent on our way. Alex reminded us of that in grown-up life: you really could test the boundaries with some things and still get away with it. We need people like that, to remind us that we don't need to be terrified into conformity. No wonder he was so popular, and that popularity was stronger nowhere more than in Ireland. They called him 'yer man' there. They loved him, and I am sure that within a few years there will be a statue or other memorial to him.

People will remember the good times because, for all Alex's ability to misbehave, he knew when he had gone too far. That's why even criticisms of him always come with a positive rejoinder. He always found a way to smooth over the situation when he needed to, because he showed a real charm when he wanted to.

Naturally, there have been many sensationalist responses to his passing, but, as a friend of Alex's, I just hope they are for the right reasons. Ken Doherty actually said just that to me just after Alex died. He rang to ask if I had heard the news and said, 'He did some horrible things, didn't he? But now when we look back on them we laugh, don't we?' It's true. At the time they seemed to be such serious things but, when we look back at many of the complaints and controversies that arose around Alex, we can see that they really didn't matter. They just didn't matter. Most of them were only slight misdemeanours, but we took them far too seriously. More than anything, he taught us that we didn't have to just go along blindly with authority. He wouldn't be controlled by anyone.

So, in those days and weeks after his passing, I looked back over my own life and saw it all with renewed clarity. If snooker did me one thing it got me out of working for a living and allowed me to avoid a life being constantly told what to do. I was free to do my own thing and to go my own way. Alex had that freedom too and, when he felt that freedom might be under threat from being even slightly curtailed by officialdom, he would kick out. Most of the rest of us would not respond that way, but a small part of us definitely admired Alex for *his* response. Even if you didn't agree with his reaction, you could identify with him.

Despite his rebellious nature he never really spoke about politics with me, or religion. He was a rebel, but not one with a specific cause of that kind. His drive, though, was to entertain – and he did that in style. For all the fuss and controversy he caused, for all the bad things he did, I still miss Alex. So does the game of snooker. Three things made snooker popular: colour television, *Pot Black* and the sheer excitement of Alex Higgins.

Will we ever see his like again?

EPILOGUE

CAMERA, ACTION!

I had to keep this story for the end.

After finding fame with *Big Break*, I started to make a snooker video each year. To bring a bit of added glitz to proceedings, I always hired a famous sidekick to appear with me. One time it was John Hollins of Chelsea; another time my friend the stuntman Rocky Taylor turned up. I also signed up Marion Ramsey, the squeaky-voiced one out of *Police Academy*, Norman Wisdom and Stanley Unwin. One year I suggested we get Alex on. I realised there was a danger that he would be a lot of trouble but it would be different and would certainly help sell more copies of the video. We offered him £5,000 for the day. I told them that the only thing was that Alex did not do trick shots. He always said, 'I do my trick shots while I'm playing.'

So I suggested we play a few frames and I said, 'You can bet your life he'll produce something special.' In one of the videos prior to this, one of the production team had been somebody who had worked with Michael Jackson. Every time I went up to ask him how he thought it was going he was positive, but he used the word 'crystal'. Well, it didn't look very 'crystal' to me.

So I said I wanted to direct the video with Alex.

I steered clear of Alex on the day when he turned up because I was wary of making him feel undermined. I was the star of this particular show, but I knew that, if he picked up that vibe, it could all go terribly wrong. As I've said, he did not enjoy being anything other than top of the bill in any situation. It could easily have gone tits up, so I kept a low profile and let the production team fawn over him. Once filming started, we began by playing a game of snooker. He got in early and potted a few balls but, basically, nothing of interest was happening. As we got near the end of a frame, I missed a red on purpose. As he was clearing up, when he got to the brown he said to me, 'Which pocket do you want the black in?'

The black was on its spot so I said, 'Middle pocket, please.'

He said, 'OK, middle pocket – and I'll do it one-handed.' If anyone has ever seen the video they can see how difficult a task it was he had just set himself. It was as good as impossible, really. However, he went through them one by one, including potting the pink most improbably. Then he still had the black to pot which, sure enough, he did one-handed into the middle pocket just as he had promised. It was breathtaking. Having potted the black he dropped his cue and flounced out of the room, like a triumphant peacock. I turned to the camera and said the first words that came into my head. 'There's only one Alex Higgins.'

After that he proceeded to play trick shots – and invent new ones. That clearance he had made had relaxed him and he was now up for anything. Mind you – the halves of lager with large crème de menthe chasers he was drinking helped.

CAREER STATISTICS

Born: 18.03.49

Turned professional: 1971

Highest Break: 142 (1985 British Open)

Career Centuries: 46

Highest ranking: 2 (1976–77, 1982–3)

CAREER HIGHS:

World Professional Snooker Champion, 1972, 1982

World Professional Snooker Championship runner-up, 1976, 1980

UK Championship winner, 1983

Benson & Hedges Masters champion, 1978, 1981

Benson & Hedges Irish Masters champion, 1989

British Gold Cup champion, 1980

Tolly Cobbold Classic champion, 1979, 1980
Irish Professional champion, 1972, 1978, 1979, 1983, 1989
Men of the Midlands champion, 1972, 1973
World Doubles champion, 1984 (with Jimmy White)
World Cup winner, 1985, 1986, 1987 (All-Ireland team)
Canadian Open champion, 1975, 1977
Pontin's Spring Open champion, 1977
Watney Open champion, 1975
Northern Ireland Amateur champion, 1968
All-Ireland Amateur champion, 1968

TRIBUTES

'I don't think you'll ever see a player in the game of snooker like the great Alex Higgins. There was just something about the way that he played the game. There was a little bit of [John] McEnroe in there. There was always going to be a little bit of controversy. If he could get the referee going a little bit he seemed to be able to play better, if he caused a little bit of havoc sometimes. But that was Alex. That made him unique.'

Dennis Taylor

'To people in the game he was a constant source of argument, he was a rebel. But to the wider public he was a breath of fresh air that drew them in to the game. He was an inspiration to my generation to take the game up. I do not think his contribution to snooker can be underestimated. He was quite a fierce competitor. He lived and breathed the game, very much a fighter on the table.'

Steve Davis

'He was a legend in the game of snooker and one of Ulster's great sportsmen. His style of play reshaped how snooker was played and his talent captivated snooker fans around the world.'

Northern Ireland Sports Minister Nelson McCausland

'Alex liked to play hard, he liked to party hard. This was one of the things that came from his great success.'

Will Robinson

'He was the original "people's champion". I have known him for nearly 40 years. He was the major reason for snooker's popularity in the early days.'

Barry Hearn

'Say what you like about Alex Higgins, but the boy had style.'

Ray Reardon

'We just remember the games when he played, everybody wanted to watch. He was exciting. Nobody knew what would happen. It was dangerous. It's a sad loss. They say every genius is bordering on mad and Alex was certainly that. You never knew if Alex was going to jump into the crowd, hit the referee, or what he would do. But he was also a fantastic cue man. He created shots that everybody now copies. All the screw shots and the backspin, it's all down to Higgins.'

Willie Thorne

'Alex was one of the real inspirations behind my getting into snooker. He is a true legend and should be for ever remembered as the finest-ever snooker player.'

Ronnie O'Sullivan

'When people write about the history of snooker they will have to devote many pages to the skills of Hurricane Higgins.'

John Higgins

'He was a very strange and complex character. You never really knew what you were going to get with him. The players, even the ones who were for many years at loggerheads with him over certain things, will still be sad to see him go because they realise what a debt they owe to him for the sport. There's never been anyone who's tried harder on a snooker table and there was never anyone who tried harder to beat throat cancer.'

John Parrott

'When he came on the scene, he was the major element in transforming snooker from a widely played folk sport into a major crowd and television attraction.'

Clive Everton

AND THE LAST WORD...

'I think I was the most natural, charismatic player who ever lifted a cue. I think my presence around the table was mesmerising at times. It captured people. I'm not saying this to bolster my own ego. It's what people tell me. People stop me in the street every day and say, "When you coming back, Alex? When you going to show these so-and-sos who claim to be snooker players how to play the game?" I say I'm not healthy enough as yet. But I'd love to.'

Alex Higgins, 2010